E S L
in America

E S L
in America
Myths and Possibilities

Edited by
Sarah Benesch
College of Staten Island
City University of New York

BOYNTON/COOK PUBLISHERS
HEINEMANN
PORTSMOUTH, NH

Boynton/Cook Publishers
A Subsidiary of
Heinemann Educational Books, Inc.
361 Hanover Street   Portsmouth, NH 03801–3959
Offices and agents throughout the world

We thank those whose works appear in this book for granting us permission to include them. We regret any oversights that may have occurred
and would be happy to rectify them in future printings.

Library of Congress Cataloging-in-Publication Data
ESL in America : myths and possibilities / edited by Sarah Benesch.
       p.   cm.
    Includes bibliographical references.
    ISBN 0-86709-266-1
    1. English language—Study and teaching—Foreign speakers.
  2. English language—Study and teaching—United States.
  I. Benesch, Sarah.
  PE1128.A2E744   1990   90–43210
  428'.007073—dc20   CIP

Printed in the United States of America
91 92 93 94 95   10 9 8 7 6 5 4 3 2 1

Contents

Part III
POSSIBILITIES

Acknowledgments

I would like to thank Bob Boynton and Elizabeth Rorschach for encouraging me to undertake this project. I thank the authors for their fine essays. Each furthers our understanding of complex problems and gives us hope that we can make a difference. Also, Barbara Danish's close readings of my chapter were invaluable.

Dawne Boyer was supportive throughout the production period. Ann Aiyawar contributed her visual intelligence to the design.

I also want to thank Ira Shor, whose critical and compassionate mind is an inspiration. Finally, I would like to acknowledge my colleagues at the College of Staten Island—David Falk, Joan Hartman, Margery Cornwell, Rose Ortiz, Bill Bernhardt, Peter Miller, Teresa O'Connor, Sita Kapadia, Maryann Castelucci, Gail Wood, Ivan Smodlaka, and Elizabeth Langan—for their commitment to our ESL population.

Introduction

Recently in a college ESL class I asked students to read and then write questions about an autobiographical essay on the internment of Japanese Americans during World War II. One student wrote, "Why did she make a story like that which could be not good for American history?" Of all the questions, the students were most interested in this one. I asked them to make two lists—one of disadvantages, the other of advantages—of learning about this part of American history. Most students had items on both lists. One advantage they cited was the necessity of learning from the mistakes of the past in order to avoid them in the future. Two students, both Palestinian, wrote about the importance of this type of knowledge in seeking solutions to current ethnic and racial problems in the United States and in their homeland. Some students, though, worried that learning about past discrimination and persecution might lead to fear and feelings of vulnerability.

Such reservations are understandable. It may be more comfortable to deny discrimination than to face it. However, ESL teachers and students alike can benefit from studying the social context in which language education takes place. This book centers on that context. Its aim is to make us more aware of our students' histories and cultures as well as their current social and economic problems so that we can develop appropriate educational solutions.

English as a second language and bilingual education are relatively young fields. The focus so far has been mainly on language, learners, and teachers, leaving the wider social, economic, and political contexts virtually unexplored. In our desire to improve teaching and learning, we have largely neglected the impact of issues, such as immigration history and law, jobs, alienation, xenophobia, and discrimination, on language acquisition. Only a few in the field (Auerbach and Burgess 1985, Cummins 1989, McKay and Wong 1988, Trueba 1989; Wallerstein 1983) have addressed questions such as these: Why did our students (or their parents) leave their native countries? What has been the U.S. government's role in the internal affairs of their home countries? What were their expectations of life in the United States? How are they being received in this country? What myths about previous generations of immigrants do we and our students live by? What are the obstacles to their academic and economic success? How can we bridge the gap between those obstacles and the ways in which we teach?

The purpose of *ESL in America: Myths and Possibilities* is to encourage greater dialogue about these questions among ourselves and with our students. All of the chapters were written especially for this book except for that of Carole Edelsky and Sarah Hudelson, reprinted here because it complements the others so well, and the student essay by Samuel Hernandez, a compelling piece about his mixed reception as a bilingual. Some of the authors are regular contributors to the ESL literature. The others come from different fields: law, sociology, school administration, and the military. The book is divided into three parts: Myths, Educational Policy, and Possibilities. Part I examines prevailing myths that affect our understanding of immigrant life, past and present. Part II contains essays on current educational policy in bilingual and ESL education with suggestions for reform. Part III contains essays about existing programs for ESL and bilingual students that address social issues as well as educational ones.

English Plus

In 1988, the Joint National Committee for Languages and the National Immigration, Refugee, and Citizenship Forum established the English Plus Information Clearinghouse (EPIC) to respond to the English Only movement, whose supporters aim to make English the official language of the United States. The strength of that movement is evident in the fact that English Only laws have been passed in sixteen states. This volume honors the notion of English Plus forwarded by EPIC: "[T]he national interest is best served when all members of our society have full access to effective opportunities to acquire strong English-language proficiency plus mastery of a second or multiple languages" (English Plus Information Clearinghouse 1988). The contributors to this volume support the idea that all those living in the United States can benefit from multilingualism and that to insist on monolingualism is to squander our precious linguistic resources (Ruiz 1988). The contributors also extend the definition of English Plus beyond questions of language acquisition and mastery to explore immigration history and law, the relationship between English and other academic areas, and the roles of community participation, counseling, and mentoring in learning English. Interferences to English learning, such as testing and tracking, are also examined.

Myths

This section provides historical background as well as legal and demographic information that defies several popular myths about current and previous generations of immigrants. It is information that we may be aware of but have not yet highlighted in our discussions of ESL and bilingual education. Juan Cartagena, in the lead chapter, explores a myth perpetuated by English Only supporters: New immigrants, unlike those who came in previous waves, don't want to learn English. ESL professionals reject that myth, knowing that new immigrants have always had to take time-consuming, blue-collar jobs and that their children were freer to learn English, at school, on the job, or from friends. Yet we don't often share this kind of information with our students, as if immigration history were unrelated to second-language acquisition. In, "English Only in the 1980s: A Product of Myths, Phobias, and Bias," Cartegena provides both historical and legal perspectives. He points out the parallels between today's English Only movement and that of the early twentieth century to show that support for language and immigration restriction has been the traditional reaction to large influxes of immigrants. Both then and more recently, attempts have been made to curtail immigrants' rights. The nativists and restrictionists have sometimes prevailed, as in the case of the immigration laws passed in the 1920s, which placed limits on the number of visas issued annually for certain national groups, and in the recent passage of English Only laws. But immigrants have also prevailed in, for example, *Myer* v. *Nebraska* and *Lau* v. *Nichols*. Cartegena explores and debunks the following myths that are now being used to rationalize English Only laws: (1) Latinos are encouraged by their community and religious leaders not to learn English. (Cartegena cites evidence to the contrary: Hispanics are on waiting lists to study English; and the traditional three-generation pattern of assimilation is being reduced to two, with the second generation losing its ability to speak Spanish); (2) English Only laws will encourage immigrants to learn English. (In fact, these laws have not led to greater educational funding or opportunity.)

"Who Are the Americans?" by Samuel Hernandez, a college student and member of the U.S. Coast Guard, also addresses the English Only question directly. This essay is a response to a videotape shown in Hernandez's ESL class that explored both sides of the English Only debate. Hernandez challenges the myth that multilingualism is divisive by showing that the country needs speakers of other languages, though that need is unacknowledged. He explains that the U.S. Coast Guard welcomes his use of Spanish when it serves their needs for translation and forbids his use of Spanish for his private purposes: "I was required to use my Spanish-speaking skills on a daily basis for the ship's mission and forbidden in other situations, such as listening to music or talking on the phone." Hernandez believes that citizenship and loyalty are not dependent on monolingualism and that bilingualism strengthens rather than divides the country.

Georges Fouron's essay "Living in Exile: The Haitian Experience," addresses the question of why groups of people from certain countries have immigrated to the United States. The conventional response is that they are seeking economic opportunity and political freedom. According to Fouron, this answer conceals a more complex socioeconomic situation.

He bases his explanation of why Haitians have migrated to the United States on the Dependency Theory of Migration. This theory hypothesizes that the movement of workers from undeveloped to developed countries is a product of the developed countries' unceasing need for profit and the attendant mechanisms that force the undeveloped countries into their sphere of influence. Fouron traces the development of Haitian dependency on the United States, beginning with the takeover of the Haitian economy by American companies and banks in the early part of the twentieth century. The dependency was reinforced, he writes, through the military occupation by American troops (1915–34) and continued with American government support of the Duvalier (Papa and Baby Doc) regimes. Haitians left their country in two waves, first in response to the brutal regimes of Papa Doc Duvalier, and then of his son. Though many of us know that Haitians sought refuge from the repressive policies of the Duvaliers, most of us know little about the roots that the American government and businesses had sunk into that country. We view Haitian migration as a flight to freedom without being fully aware of our own country's role in the political and economic oppression that caused people to flee. The second part of Fouron's article deals with Haitians' reception in this country. Here we have another myth exploded: Haitians have not been embraced but rather scorned because they are black and because they are immigrants. As Fouron concludes, "While capitalism produces the factors that encourage and foster migration, immigrants are made to feel unwanted in the host society. The painful experience of exile is brought to reality by the position of the Haitian immigrants as blacks in a staunchly class-structured society motivated by deep-seated racial and ethnic considerations."

Philip Tajitsu Nash, in "ESL and the Myth of the Model Minority," challenges another popular myth, this one perpetuated by the mass media and some educators: Asian immigrants are intellectually superior and more ambitious than other groups of immigrants. First, Nash points out that Asian immigrants are a diverse group with different histories, languages, and cultures. Next, he traces the history of discrimination against Asian immigrants, showing the progression from an earlier myth, "the yellow peril," to the current one, "the model minority." Nash also provides a helpful framework for studying the impact, contributions, and difficulties of the new immigrants from Asia. He makes a distinction between "brain drain" immigrants, educated professionals, and those who were forced by the Vietnam War and economic conditions to emigrate (Fouron would call this dependency migration.) The myth of the model minority exists, Nash claims, because of the achievements of the first group. They arrive with degrees and/or capital, which allow them to pursue advanced education or start small businesses. This rapid entry into the mainstream seems miraculous (How do they *do* it?) until we begin to understand that some immigrants arrive with educational and economic tools that smooth their path.

Though Nash does not belittle the achievements of educated, middle-class immigrants, he cautions us not to ignore the investment made by their home countries in their development and not to compare them to Asians who arrive with little prior education and capital. The myth of the model minority does not help either group of Asian immigrants. It provokes envy in their native counterparts and creates unfair expectations that all Asians (and other American minorities), no matter what their educational and economic background, can make it on their own, by their own bootstraps.

Educational Policy

The two chapters in this section analyze current trends in bilingual and ESL education and suggest reforms that would make teaching more responsive to particular social and academic conditions. Both articles favor locally-developed solutions to complex educational problems over top-down, bureaucratic solutions. In "ESL on Campus: Questioning Testing and Tracking Policies," I describe the present policy of many colleges to segregate ESL students in test-driven, multitracked remedial programs. This practice is based on two myths: (1) reading and writing can be tested and taught as a set of decontextualized skills; (2) homogeneous classes can be achieved by testing and tracking students. I challenge these assumptions and give examples of unsound teaching that results from such beliefs. ESL faculty who teach in programs governed by testing and tracking must juggle the academic needs of the students—to learn to read and write critically—with a bureaucratic policy for handling large groups of students—mass testing and tracking. In this article I consider ways to replace obsolete language testing, placement, and teaching methods with a more appropriate pedagogy—heterogeneous ESL classes linked to "content" courses. Colleges adopting such a policy would admit ESL students as full-fledged members of the academic community rather than as remedial students who must pass skills tests and classes unrelated to their academic interests.

Next, Carole Edelsky and Sarah Hudelson, in "Contextual Complexities: Written Language Policies for Bilingual Programs," demonstrate that given the lack of uniformity in language and dialect groups across schools it is inadvisable to offer a single policy of written language instruction for all bilingual students. To illustrate the layers of linguistic and educational complexity that policymakers face, they cite a hypothetical school district in which there are immigrant students from various areas of the world (Latin America, the Caribbean, Asia, Europe) with different levels of literacy in their native languages and different immigration statuses, from second-generation Cubans to recently arrived Southeast Asian refugees. Why should we expect a single federal, state, city, or district policy to be appropriate for all the schools of that district, each with its own mix of languages, cultures, and educational backgrounds? The authors call on policymakers to provide broad guidelines that would allow educators to make decisions at the school level. They suggest basing local decisions on the following information: (1) an understanding of current work in written language acquisition; (2) an awareness of language resources in the community; (3) knowledge of local beliefs and attitudes about writing and written products; and (4) knowledge of the place of writing in the community and of possible effects of learning to write on community members.

Possibilities

The chapters in this section describe locally-developed language and literacy programs that are responsive to the social, economic, political, and academic needs of their students. Each program serves a different population—refugee families, immigrant families, ESL college students, and American-born language minority college students—in different instructional settings. Yet each is based on the assumption that language instruction is only one factor that influences a program's development. Because the programs were shaped with local conditions in mind, they are appropriate to the students they serve.

William Waxman, principal of the Garfield School in Revere, Massachusetts, describes the ways in which his school transformed itself to welcome an influx of refugee students. Garfield School teachers, students, parents, and administrators prepared themselves for the arrival of a large group of Cambodian families in the community and school by learning about Cambodian culture and history. When the refugee families arrived, the school provided such services as housing assistance and translators. The children were assigned American-born "buddies" and, eventually, two-way bilingual, bicultural programs were established. Waxman tells the history of the changes made in the community and school to embrace the new members, who were viewed as a gift rather than a burden.

Like Waxman, Elsa Auerbach and Loren McGrail believe that education cannot be divorced from the social context of students' lives. In "Rosa's Challenge: Connecting Classrooms and Community Contexts," they describe a family literacy program that departs from the usual focus on teaching parents how to help their children perform better in school, what the authors call a "from-the-school-to-the-community-and-family model." Instead, they allowed the conditions of their students' lives to shape the program, a "from-the-family-and-community-to-the-school model." To respond to local conditions, they accepted into the program not only members of nuclear families but members of extended families and caretakers. And they organized classes to accommodate the linguistic complexities they discovered. Some classes served members of a single language group while others had students from as many as twenty-six language groups. They also invited teachers and students to create an "emergent, negotiated curriculum" through "ongoing, collaborative investigation of the students' lives," using the participatory or problem-posing approach developed by Paulo Freire. Auerbach and McGrail describe the activities the teachers and students engage in: (1) finding the students' themes and issues; (2) extending those themes through the use of pictures, published texts, and teacher and student-generated texts; (3) action, such as student participation in class, in the program, and in the community; and (4) evaluation. The chapter ends with an excerpt from McGrail's journal that describes the evolution of the participatory cycle in one of her classes.

In "A Collaborative Model for Empowering Nontraditional Students," Teri Haas, Trudy Smoke, and José Hernández describe their jointly-developed program for minority and immigrant college students. The authors point out that these students are often the first in their families to go to college and that they enter with a great deal of motivation to succeed. They soon become discouraged, however, by repeated failure on placement tests and by being tracked into remedial courses. Acknowledging that these students need practice reading, writing, and studying, yet believing that these are not skills to be learned out of context, the authors linked their developmental writing, ESL writing, and social science courses. The theme of the social science course, "Conquered Peoples in America," is particularly appropriate for nontraditional students. This course explores the history and consequences of American expansion in the nineteenth century. The students learn about the common experiences of Native Americans, African Americans, Mexican Americans, and Asian/Pacific Americans, all victims of the European conquest of the Americas and the subsequent expansion of the U.S. domain. According to the authors, students of different national and cultural backgrounds who at the beginning of the course had avoided one another began to draw closer as they learned that their peoples shared a history of conquest and colonization. The benefits of joining developmental writing, ESL writing, and "Conquered Peoples in America" were that: (1) ESL and minority students studied together (they are usually sorted into parallel tracks); (2) listening to lectures, taking notes, discussing, reading and writing were carried out in an academic context rather than in a remedial, skills-based context; (3) the writing assignments, based on "Conquered Peoples" topics, allowed the students to explore those topics more fully; and (4) students learned that their histories are significant and worthy of scholarly study. The solution presented by Haas, Smoke, and Hernández was developed locally but may serve as a model of collaboration across disciplines and cultures.

This volume, then, looks not only at the language classroom but also at the world outside to discover how education is shaped by problems in the larger society. To help our students achieve their goals, we need to understand their expectations and how and why those expectations are being met or stymied. By becoming more aware of the sociopolitical dimension of second language teaching as well as of models that have taken this dimension into account, we will be able to make more informed pedagogical decisions.

References

Auerbach, E.R., and D. Burgess 1985. The hidden curriculum of survival ESL. *TESOL Quarterly* 19(3): 475–95

Cummins. J. 1989. *Empowering minority students.* Sacramento: California Association for Bilingual Education.

English Plus Information Clearinghouse launched: 1988. *EPIC Events* 1 (1): 1.

McKay, S. L., and S. C. Wong, eds. 1988. *Language diversity: problem or resource?* New York: Newbury House.

Ruiz, R. 1988. Orientations in language planning. In McKay, S. L., and S. C. Wong, *Language diversity: problem or resource?* New York: Newbury House.

Trueba, H. 1989. *Raising silent voices: Educating linguistic minorities for the 21st century.* New York: Newbury House.

Wallerstein, N. 1983. *Language and culture in conflict: Problem posing in the ESL classroom.* Reading, MA: Addison-Wesley.

I

MYTHS

1

English Only in the 1980s
A Product of Myths, Phobias, and Bias

Juan Cartagena
*The Commonwealth of Puerto Rico's Department of
Puerto Rican Community Affairs*

Introduction

A Puerto Rican woman casts a vote in Jersey City after reading a ballot initiative printed in Spanish. A public health brochure on teen pregnancy is distributed in Brooklyn in Haitian Creole. A bilingual—English, Mandarin—ad in a subway car announces low-cost checking available at a popular bank in Manhattan. A resident of Hamtramck, Michigan, fondly recalls the words of the Pope as he addressed this city in Polish in 1987. A faded wooden sign in Monsey, New York, marks the entrance to the city hall in English and Hebrew.

These are some images of today's America. They are also, in large part, the images of yesterday's America. Each of them is threatened by the present call to declare English the only language that governments can use in the United States. As the present-day nativism starts to approach the fervor of the early twentieth century, three things are certain. First, the call for new laws is aimed at a different set of immigrants and migrants in the United States, a group much darker in complexion. Second, the present call is a naked attempt to arrest growing political influence by linguistic minorities in the country. And, third, the present debate stands on a foundation of myths, phobias, and bias.

What follows is an exploration of these themes and a discussion about a small but influential segment of the population that has confronted language restrictionist policies for nearly a century: the Puerto Ricans. Initially, however, a discussion of the historical underpinning of language policy in the United States is in order.

Historical Points in U.S. Language Policy

"The protection of the Constitution extends to all, to those who speak other languages as well as those born with English on the tongue" (Myer *v.* Nebraska).

The history of U.S. language policy shows a strange quilt of trends and movements that embrace, and at times reject, accommodation of other languages in public life. This history, however, discloses that there has always been resistance to creating an exclusively monolingual society in the United States. Instead, a cyclical or spiral pattern best describes the nation's language policy. One lesson that history teaches us, however, is clear: the English only movement of the 1980s is not new in America.

Founded upon the principle of ensuring life, liberty, and the pursuit of happiness, the United States contained a multiplicity of languages during the colonial and revolutionary periods. The numerous Native American languages and the arrival of the Spanish in North America before the first English settlement may have forced a more accommodationist view of language policy in this country. That is to say, the country was new and attractive to the Germans, the French, the Dutch, and many others. Thus, for example, the Articles of Confederation, the precursor of the Constitution, was translated into German to attract the support of German residents in a number of American colonies (Kloss 1977).

More importantly, the Constitution did not establish English as the official language of the country. The choice apparently was deliberate, as even a proposal to establish a governmental body to regulate the English language was rejected by the Continental Congress. Political liberty, not cultural homogeneity, was much more important to the framers to the Constitution (Crawford 1989a).

As the country progressed in the 1800s, three distinct national-origin groups were woven into its fabric. Each left its mark on U.S. language policy. First, the Germans quickly became the largest language minority group in the colonies, and, subsequently, the most important language minority group to have an impact upon this country's language policies. Germans created their own public schools to preserve their language and successfully thwarted attempts to establish English schools in the same areas. These practices made them the subject of scorn and the abuse by language restrictionists. Second, the termination of the Mexican-American War in 1848 resulted in over 75,000 Mexicans becoming U.S. citizens by operation of the Treaty of Guadalupe Hidalgo (Castellanos 1983). The Treaty preserved the right of these settlers to their land and arguably to their language and culture (Cartagena, Kaimowitz, and Perez 1983) as Mexicans throughout what is now the American Southwest became citizens without having to demonstrate English proficiency. Third, in 1898 the United States invaded Puerto Rico and, in 1917, imposed U.S. citizenship on all Puerto Ricans. Once again, English proficiency was not a precondition to citizenship. Neither the Mexicans nor the Puerto Ricans, therefore, fit the typical immigration stereotype. Bridges remain behind them. Ellis Island and the Statue or Liberty have not been their gateways.

In the mid-nineteenth century, the first wave of language restrictionist policies began to take hold. With the coming of large numbers of Irish and Italian immigrants, descendants of the English settlers began to harbor suspicions and resentments against these people and their Catholicism (San Miguel 1986). The arrival of Mexicans and Asians added more peoples with different languages. At first Chinese were recruited to work on the railroads, but subsequently they were barred from the United States for decades (see Nash, this volume). All new territorial acquisitions, such as the Philippines and Puerto Rico, were forced to use English; public and private schools were ordered to use English as the language of instruction; and some states began to declare English as the required language for public affairs.

But the heyday of language restrictionist policies arrived in the early twentieth century. More than ever, the tie between language restrictions and immigration restrictions dominated the political scene. In 1920, Congress enacted sweeping immigration laws that placed national origin quotas on the number of visas issued annually. The quotas favored England and other northern European countries at the expense of southern European countries. The Ku Klux Klan, whose membership exceeded four million in 1925, proclaimed its mission to save the "Nordic race" from the onslaught of Jews, Slavs, and Catholics (Wittke 1939). States began to criminalize the use of German in all areas of public life, including on city streets and the telephone. Over 18,000 people in the Midwest were charged with violations of these laws (Crawford 1989a, 23). Anti-German hysteria peaked with the enactment of such laws and the country's entry into World War I in 1917. Increasingly, the arrival of Jews, Italians, and Slavs led to continued suspicions over their loyalty to the country and their capacity for change.

> Old-stock Americans, which now included children of earlier waves of immigrants, believed that the "new immigrants" lacked the assimilative qualities which the "old immigrants" possessed. Further, new immigrants were thought to lack a democratic background and understanding of American institutions, as well as to contribute to vagrancy and crime (San Miguel 1986, 13).

In 1923, the Supreme Court effectively ended this first wave of nativism, at least with respect to language-restrictionist laws. The Court ruled in *Myer* v. *Nebraska* that states could not, under the Constitution, criminally punish residents for teaching foreign languages to students in the schools. The defendant in this case was a private-school teacher who taught German to a young student whose parents hoped would learn the language in order to read their German Bible. Nebraska authorities tried to persuade the Supreme Court, unsuccessfully, that the state's language restriction law was constitutional because Germans had proven that they could not be assimilated into the American mainstream and because their continued use of German indicated a disloyalty to the United States (Trasvina 1988). The Court rejected these arguments, and its ruling affected the laws of over twenty states that similarly sought to outlaw the use of foreign languages (Combs and Trasvina 1986). In addition to the Midwestern states, Vermont, Connecticut, New Hampshire, and Massachusetts had enacted laws restricting the use of French in public and private schools at this time (San Miguel 1986).

The period between the 1920s and 1980 contained other important events that shaped U.S. language policies. Immigration restrictions were lessened somewhat with the elimination of the discriminatory national origin quotas in 1965. However, the implementation of English proficiency requirements for naturalization gained steam. Additional events that shaped language policy during this period have been identified (Cartagena 1989) to include: (1) the ratification by the United States of the United Nations Charter, which includes "language" as an impermissible basis of differentiation alongside "race" and "religion"; (2) the passage of the National Defense Education Act of 1958 in response to Russia's Sputnik launch, which financed the teaching of foreign languages in public schools; (3) the Voting Rights Act of 1965 and amendments to that law in 1970. The original Act exempted Puerto Ricans from English only literacy requirements for voter registration and an amendment mandated bilingual assistance in the voting process for all major language minorities; and (4) the upsurge in bilingual education as a result of the 1974 *Lau* v. *Nichols* Supreme Court opinion and the Equal Education Opportunity Act of 1974, which prohibited states from discriminating against students by failing to remove language barriers that may impede educational progress.

These events reflect a true contradiction in the United States. At times, foreign language learning has been promoted and respected. At times, English has consciously not been used as a precondition to certain rights and programs. Yet citizenship, and loyalty in the eyes of many, is still conditioned on knowledge of English, and many youngsters are still ridiculed and punished in schools for speaking Spanish.

By the 1980s the domestic economic situation, immigration patterns and, as in the early 1900s, an upsurge in xenophobic attitudes refueled controversy over the language policies of the nation. In no uncertain terms, the proponents of the new English Language Amendment repeated the same observations about Latinos in the United States that were used against previous immigrant groups. The present English only movement can only be understood in this context.

The Present English Only Movement

> "'We, the people of the United States, in order to form a more perfect union...' U.S. English" (U.S. English, Inc., motto).

"...put a gun to their heads, and if they say 'don't shoot', we'll know they can speak English" (*Wall Street Journal* 1986).

U.S. English, Inc., and English First are the organizational leaders of the current English only movement. These two organizations have financed the current drive at the state level to declare English the official language of each state. Their aim, however, is clear. Only an amendment to the U.S. Constitution will suffice.

Like so many of its predecessors, the movement is aimed at immigrants. Note the following reference to our latest immigrants in this letter from English First:

> They never become productive members of American society. They remain stuck in a linguistic and economic ghetto, many living off welfare and costing working Americans millions of tax dollars every year (English First a).

Founded in 1983, U.S. English was created by former Senator S. I. Hayakawa and Dr. John H. Tanton as an "offshoot" of the Federation of American Immigration Reform (Crawford 1989a). Around this time, Senator Hayakawa introduced, for the first time in American history, an amendment to the U.S. Constitution to declare English as the country's official language.

U.S. English, Inc., has developed numerous objectives during its short existence. The organization is committed to the promotion of the "use of English in political and economic life" while rejecting "all manifestations of cultural or linguistic chauvinism" (U.S. English a). Thus it calls for:

- Adoption of a Constitutional amendment to establish English as the official language of the United States.
- Repeal of laws mandating multilingual ballots and voting materials.
- Restriction of government funding for bilingual education to short-term transitional programs only.
- Universal enforcement of the English language and civics requirement for naturalization.

Not obvious in these stated objectives are the immediate targets of U.S. English, which are quite different:

> At various times, leaders of U.S. English have advocated elimination of bilingual 911 operators and health services, endorsed English only rules in the workplace, petitioned the Federal Communications Commission to limit foreign-language broadcasting, protested Spanish-language menus at McDonald's, and

opposed Pacific Bell's *Paginas Amarillas en Espanol* and customer assistance in Chinese (Crawford 1989a, 55).

Similarly, "English First" was founded to add the English Language Amendment to the U.S. Constitution. Its aim is to stop the "dangerous spread of 'bilingualism' in our society," by ending bilingual ballots and other bilingual programs (English First a).

Recently, however, startling revelations have surfaced concerning the largest of these proponents, U.S. English, Inc. A 1986 memorandum written by cofounder John Tanton regarding the consequences of Latino immigration in the United States revealed clear, racist motives by this influential chairman. In his memorandum, Tanton decried the "cultural threats" posed by continued Latino immigration to include Latinos' "low educability," high drop-out rates, failure to use birth control, tradition of the *mordida* (bribe), "lack of involvement in public affairs," and allegiance to Roman Catholicism that did not respect this country's separation of church and state (Tanton 1986). In a plea for action by the "majority" not unlike the white supremacist calls in the 1920s, Tanton states:

> *Gobernar es poblar* translates "to govern is to populate." …Will the present majority peaceably hand over its political power to a group that is simply more fertile? …As Whites see their power and control over their lives declining, will they simply go quietly into the night? Or will there be an explosion? We are building a deadly disunity. All great empires disintegrate; we want stability.

Simultaneously with the disclosure of the Tanton memo, financial data revealed that the financiers of U.S. English included heiress Cordelia Scaife May and the Pioneer Fund. The former financed the distribution of a French novel in which third world immigrants invade and destroy Europe. The latter is dedicated to white racial superiority and eugenics (Crawford 1988).

Despite these gaffes, U.S. English continues to push for language restrictionist policies while trying to shy away from their reactionary image. Linda Chavez, their Hispanic president, resigned in the wake of the disclosures, calling the Tanton view "repugnant…anti-Hispanic and anti-Catholic." Chavez, who had previously denied, adamantly, that the English only movement was racist, conceded that their legal initiatives "do polarize the community, whether intentionally or not, and this is not in the interest of bringing Hispanics into the mainstream" (Crawford 1989b). Similarly, Walter Cronkite resigned at the same time from the notable U.S. English advisory board, becoming the second such advisory board member to quit in recent years over the direction of the organization. Author Norman Cousins resigned in October 1986 just before the election in which the California English only referendum appeared, stating that "there is a very real danger" that Proposition 63 would cause Latinos and other racial minorities to be "disadvantaged, denigrated, and demeaned" (*Los Angeles Times* b). Other members of U.S. English who continue to serve on the advisory board despite calls for their resignations from opponents of English only measures include Walter Annenberg, Jacques Barzun, Saul Bellow, Alistair Cooke, Barbara Mujica, Norman Podhoretz, and Arnold Schwarzenegger.

Nevertheless, the English only movement is quite alive today, in part because of the simplicity of its seemingly innocuous message. Proponents of English only call for laws to declare English the official language of the state, or, alternatively, the country. It is difficult to argue with this simple proposition without explaining that such laws will establish English as the *only* language that is sanctioned by the government. Accordingly, other languages will be outlawed, to the detriment of those who need such services. On the other hand, some modern variations of English only legislation are not so innocent. Arizona's referendum, which passed by the slimmest of margins in November 1988, requires all state and municipal employees to conduct their business in English—in effect, an English only workrule for all state employees. In 1989, the county legislature in Suffolk Country, New York, just barely defeated a similar proposal that would have even required all contractors and subcontractors of the county to conduct their business only in English. All this in a country where 98 percent of all its residents, according to the 1980 census, understand and speak English!

In actuality, the present call for language restrictionist legislation preys upon the dominant culture's fears and misconceptions about the country's language minorities. Three myths underlie the restrictionist agenda.

"Our grandparents got by without special treatment or materials, why can't you?"

Proponents of language restrictionist laws have glorified the otherwise traumatic experiences of their forefathers in the debate over language restrictionist laws. In effect, they have to, for this would create imaginary divisions between "older" immigrants and "newer" immigrants. Such divisions can only support their call for drastic action. Former Senator Hayakawa has made the distinction quite clear: "At one time, most immigrants' first task was to learn English. This is no longer an accepted fact" (Hayakawa 1983). Other leaders of the English only movement have a remarkable way of basing public policy on their own personal experiences. For example, Texas legislator Jim Horn can somehow divine that English was so easily accessible for his forebears: "I don't know about your forefathers but when mine came to America, the first thing they did was learn English" (English First a). Larry Pratt, president of English First, similarly shares his view about the complex issues of language acquisition through the eyes of his Panamanian spouse (English First b).

Despite these subjective claims, historically the immigrant experience has not been a bed of roses in the United States, and English acquisition did not come about so easily. Nor were immigrants able to sacrifice getting a job or a home to immediately learn English. Immigrant children also bore the burdens and traumas of the immigrant experience. "A large percentage of immigrant children—Armenian, Irish, Italian, Polish, German, Russian, Chinese, and Mexican—who arrived at school not understanding or speaking English failed in school and, in failing, suffered a serious loss of self-esteem and unrealized potential" (Jimenez 1987). These patterns were officially documented by the Federal Immigration Commission (Dillingham Commission) report in 1911, which set the stage for national origin quotas in our immigration laws. The Dillingham Commission found that 51 percent of German students were two grades behind their peers; 60 percent of the Russian students were equally behind as were 70 percent of the Italian students. In those days, government officials disclosed their prejudices openly: the newer immigrants were considered to be "less intelligent, less willing to learn English, or did not have the intention of settling in the United States" (*ibid.*).

In this context, the attempt to paint divisions between older and newer immigrants is disingenuous. As will be discussed below, Latinos and Asians are acquiring English at the same rates, if not faster, than previous immigrant communities. The division, however, does serve a function, as English speakers who support English only do so believing that there's something wrong with Latinos, Asians, Haitians, and others today.

"You people don't want to learn English."

Assimilation is a recurrent theme in the arguments posed by current language restrictionists. U.S. English alleges that Latinos refuse to learn English. Assimilation by operation of law is their solution. Again, another wedge is placed between Latinos and all other immigrant groups. Thus U.S. English states:

> The assimilative process is not working as well as it did during previous periods of large-scale immigration. Several studies, all of them undertaken under Hispanic sponsorship, indicate growing attachment to Spanish over time, and increasing separation from the mainstream (U.S. English b).

This line of argument continues by setting up Latino leaders as a straw man that must be overcome in order to save the flock. For example, Hayakawa asserts: "Nor does Hispanic leadership seem to be alarmed that large populations of Mexican Americans, Cubans, and Puerto Ricans do not speak English and have no intention of learning" (Hayakawa 1985, 12). His counterpart, John Tanton, assumes the role of liberator when he proclaims: "The way to demean minority citizens is to keep them in language ghettos, where they can be controlled by self-serving ethnic politicians" (*Los Angeles Times* b).

Quite the opposite is true for Latinos in this country. Latinos are acquiring English at the same rate, if not faster, than other immigrant groups. As for large numbers of those who do not want to know English, the words of T. Edward Hollander, Chancellor of Higher Education in New Jersey, ring true: "There is no such person in this country who doesn't understand the value of knowledge and understanding of English as a key to individual success and achievement" (Hollander 1987).

No "study" that U.S. English can cite can refute what has been already documented thoroughly. Recent studies by Calvin Veltman in this area have been highlighted by Crawford (1989a). Veltman concluded that among Spanish speakers, the shift to English dominance is already approaching a two-generation pattern in virtually the entire country as compared to the three-generation pattern exhibited by other immigrants. The typical three-generation pattern describes language acquisition over generations of newcomers. Thus the first generation arrives in the United States proficient in their native language and generally does not obtain full English proficiency. Their children, the second generation, typically acquire English and maintain their native language. The grandchildren, however, become proficient only in English and lose the language of their parents and grandparents. In 1988, Veltman also found that seven out of ten children of Hispanic immigrants were English speakers, and in 1983 he found that bilingual education has no measurable impact on slowing the rate of acquiring English. Far from English being in danger, Veltman found that other languages in the United States are in peril. In 1984, a National Opinion Research Center survey showed that 81 percent of Hispanics believe that speaking and understanding English is a very important obligation (American Jewish Committee 1987). And in 1985, a Rand Corporation study found that 90 percent of first-generation Mexican Americans are proficient in English and over half of the second generation can only speak English (*New York Times* 1986)!

Adult English classes attract literally thousands of Latinos for registration. In 1986 in Los Angeles, 40,000 were turned away from English as a second language classes offered by the Los Angeles Unified School District (*Los Angeles Times* b). In New York, thousands more are on waiting lists. And by 1989, with the passage of the Immigration Reform and Control Act, Latinos and others were competing for scarce seats in English classes (English Plus Information Clearinghouse 1988). This was caused by the Immigration Act's requirement that English proficiency be demonstrated for all applicants for legal permanent residency under the Act's amnesty provisions. Thousands of immigrants are now in need of more English classes where there are none. Facts like these led Norman Cousins to resign from U.S. English and state:

> Not until we provide educational facilities for all who are now standing in line waiting to take lessons in English should we presume to pass judgment on the non-English-speaking people in our midst (*Los Angeles Times* b).

Latinos, therefore, do not need U.S. English to liberate them. They have done it themselves.

"Laws declaring English the official language will help today's immigrants learn English."

Perhaps the most deceiving element in the jargon of English only proponents is the representation that these proposed laws will assist non-English speakers learn the language. English First has stated that:

> The ELA [English Language Amendment] ensures equal opportunity for all to progress economically, *to learn English as quickly as possible,* and to be equally and justly served by a government that refuses to discriminate against those who do not speak one of its favored languages (English First c).

Recently, a representative of U.S. English asserted that the passage of English-as-official-language laws permitted the financing of English classes, implying that the latter could not have occurred otherwise (Acle 1989). The votes in favor of official English laws in Florida in 1988 and in California in 1986 demonstrated that many Latino voters thought such laws would result in increasing English classes for adults.

The sad truth is that laws declaring English the official language of any state do not address the overwhelming problem of providing educational opportunities. "It [the English Language Amendment] will not provide for one more textbook, one more teacher, one more aide, or one more classroom to teach English," states the National Education Association (1988). U.S. English refused to support the English Proficiency Bill sponsored by the Congressional Hispanic Caucus in 1987, which eventually provided a mere $4.8 million for adult English as a second language classes. These developments led many observers to question the motives of the language restrictionists. In 1987, Teachers of English to Speakers of Other Languages noted that the money used by these English only proponents could have been better spent to teach English (Crawford 1989a).

Puerto Ricans: A Community Against English Only.

The Puerto Rican community in the United States has had direct experience with language restrictionist policies since 1898. It is a community that is increasingly bilingual. It is a community that has shaped language policy at all levels of government in order to guarantee equal rights to all. Puerto Ricans know all too well that the imposition of English only policies does not work.

Approximately 2.7 million Puerto Ricans live in the continental United States. As with all other nationalities that have arrived in the country, Puerto Ricans know the value of learning English and see its acquisition, generally, as an asset and a necessity (Pedraza 1985). Equally important, in New York City, the largest Puerto Rican community in the United States, Puerto Ricans are neither abandoning their mother tongue nor resisting English. A higher proportion of Puerto Ricans—91 percent—still speak Spanish at home, compared to all other Latino groups. Simultaneously, a higher proportion of Puerto Ricans—70 percent—speak English "well" and "very well," as compared to all other Latino groups (Rodriguez 1989, 30). Thus, for this population, especially its youth, there is no contradiction in being bilingual, bicultural, and American (*ibid.*, 149).

It is because Puerto Ricans have experienced an attempt to impose English only policies in their native land that, today, they are at the forefront of the struggle to stop U.S. English and English First (Cartagena 1989). Spanish was Puerto Rico's national language for 390 years at the time of the U.S. takeover of the island in 1898. A year later, the hand-picked American in charge of the island's education system ridiculed Puerto Ricans by proclaiming that their Spanish was a patois that possessed no literature or value (Garcia Martinez 1981). This attitude of ridicule, contempt, and superiority permeated the actions taken by the United States against the colony of Puerto Rico. Overnight, English became the medium of instruction in all public schools. American cultural and historical heroes replaced Puerto Rican culture and values. As Puerto Ricans struggled to gain some measure of control over their educational system, they organized all teachers, administrators, and legislators to pass laws to regain Spanish as the medium of instruction. In 1946, President Truman vetoed such legislation, thus becoming the first president to veto legislation originating in Puerto Rico (San Juan Cafferty and Rivera Martinez 1981). Finally, in 1949 Spanish was used as the language of instruction in the public schools.

This attempt at "Anglicization" (Rodriguez Bou 1966) had severe consequences: a marked erosion of Puerto Rican culture, an 80 percent dropout rate in Puerto Rico's public schools at the time, and *no full English proficiency* (Zentella 1987).

An analysis of the current debate over language policy can not be complete without addressing the relationship of these policies to the Puerto Rican question. History is not the only reason for focusing on this population. The fact is that Puerto Ricans, American citizens since 1917, have been largely ignored in the debate. The Puerto Rican experience in the United States is one that demonstrates how political power and litigation strategy can result in securing services and programs in languages other than English. This benefits all language minorities. It also provokes action to disempower the Puerto Rican community as in the drive to make English the only official language. There is little doubt left that the current language-restrictionist debate is really an anti-Spanish debate. The items cited above concerning the major actors in U.S. English and English First support this as do the written materials produced by these proponents. Some of these briefing packets are clearly directed at Spanish speakers and denounce the presence of Spanish broadcasting, the proximity of Spanish speaking countries of origin for today's immigrants, and the motives of Latino leaders (*ibid.*) The atmosphere of intolerance that English only supporters have created affects many areas of Puerto Rican life. Adult literacy classes in Puerto Rican neighborhoods have also felt the pressure to conduct literacy classes solely in English. Fortunately, many have resisted (Torruellas 1989).

Puerto Ricans and other Latinos played a leading role in forcing Congress to acknowledge that the electoral and political process, when conducted only in English, discriminates and diminishes political participation by American citizens. Bilingual voting materials have played a significant role in assisting these communities and in increasing their political participation. In 1984, a survey conducted by the Southwest Voter Participation Project, found in four states that 30 percent of the Mexicans responding would not have registered to vote had it not been for bilingual voting materials. Another survey published in 1988 by the Commonwealth of Puerto Rico found that 29 percent of all Puerto Ricans surveyed in New York City listed language barriers, such as the consistent failure to secure sufficient bilingual assistance at the polls, as an impediment to voting.

The bilingual ballot and bilingual voter-registration materials are clear targets for elimination by U.S. English and others. Thus the stage is set. By eliminating the ballot in a language that many, but not all, Puerto Ricans can understand, political power is diminished. None of today's language restrictionists have addressed the fact that Puerto Ricans, as U.S. citizens from a Spanish-speaking territory, must continue to receive various services in Spanish.

Instead, the only official mention of Puerto Ricans occurs when the island's political status is at issue. The people of Puerto Rico and the U.S. Congress are beginning to debate a proposed plebiscite on the island's political future that will include the options of independence, statehood, or continued commonwealth status. In attempting a preemptive strike, U.S. English, Inc., testified before the congressional hearings to, in effect, place conditions on statehood, should it be chosen by the Puerto Ricans:

> ...during these historical debates, we feel it would be badly mis-leading for the people of Puerto Rico to vote in the plebiscite thinking that any language, other than English, can be the official language of a State of the Union (U.S. English c).

Once again, an attempt is made to impose English on Puerto Rico. These machinations by U.S. English are made with the full knowledge that they are better equipped to influence a Senate committee than to convince the residents of Puerto Rico. By using this route, the language restriction-ists expose the fact that they seek to control by force and numbers a de-cision that is often left to the local electorate. For example, New Mexico has Spanish and English as official languages, and Hawaii has Hawaiian and English as official languages. Should statehood befall Puerto Rico, it would be spared this liberty, according to U.S. English.

Puerto Ricans know better. They will continue to ensure that out-side forces will not impose language and cultural norms against their will. And in the United States they will continue to uphold the principle that differentiation on the basis of language is a violation of basic human rights.

Conclusion

The present English only movement has garnered the support of sixteen states that have passed English-as-official-language laws. In recent years an equivalent number of states have rejected such laws. The debate, as demonstrated on recent television shows, becomes emotional. Revela-tions about the founders and financing of U.S. English, Inc., continue to add more fire to the dispute over the consequences of these unneces-sary laws. In a world of increasing interdependence, the United States may be taking a step backwards. Linguistic divisions tend to lead to po-litical conflict whenever the dominant group seeks to impose its view on all members of a society and arrests the development and empowerment of minority groups. This is exactly what is occurring in the United States. Instead of unifying the country over issues such as liberty and prosperi-ty, today's language restrictionists are doing the opposite: "Officializa-tion of English is more likely to create language conflict and to politicize language differences than to avoid it [*sic*]" (Guy 1988, 5)

As it strives to legislate uniformity, the English Language Amend-ment threatens our beliefs in diversity, tolerance, and individual liberty (Ruiz 1989). The following passage from the Puerto Rican sociolinguist,

Ana Celia Zentella, raises what may be the ultimate question posed by the English only movement:

> How does what starts out as an innocent "We just want to help everyone learn English so that we may communicate and they can succeed," turn into the odious impugning of the patriotism of those who support the rights of language minorities? It is because language is not the real issue, but a smokescreen for the fact that the U.S. has not resolved the inequality that exists, and finds it convenient to blame linguistic differences. The root of the problem lies in an inability to accept an expanded definition of what it is to be an American today (1987, 21).

References

Acle, L. 1989. Interview with author and others on WWOR-TV "People Are Talking," Mar. 13, 1989.

American Jewish Committee. 1987. "English as the official language" policy statement (on file with author).

Cartagena, J. 1989. English Only jamas. *Centro Bulletin,* 2:5 (Spring 1989) (Centro de Estudios Puertorriquenos, Hunter College, New York, NY).

Cartagena, J., G. Kaimowitz, and I. Perez. 1983. U.S. language policy: Where do we go from here? Paper presented at conference, El Espanol en los Estados Unidos IV, Hunter College, New York, NY.

Castellanos, D. 1983. *The best of two worlds: Bilingual-bicultural education in the U.S.* Trenton, NJ: New Jersey State Dept. of Education.

Combs, M. C. and J. Trasvina, 1986. Legal implications of the English Language Amendment. In *The "English Plus" project.* Washington, DC: League of United Latin American Citizens.

Crawford, J. 1988. What's behind English Only II: Strange bedfellows. *Hispanic Link Weekly Report,* Oct. 31, 1988, p. 3.

————. 1989a. *Bilingual education: History, politics, theory and practice.* Trenton, NJ: Crane Publishing Co.

————. 1989b. Linda Chavez gives it to us in plain English. *Hispanic Link Weekly Report,* June 19, 1989, p. 3.

English First. Soliciting letter by Jim Horn. Undated (on file with author).

————. Soliciting letter by Larry Pratt. Nov. 19, 1986 (on file with author).

————. Remarks by Larry Pratt. Undated (on file with author).

English Plus Information Clearinghouse. 1988. EPIC events, Mar./Apr. 1988.

Guy G., 1988. Presentation on a panel on the International Situation and Comparative Analysis of Language Policy, at the Conference on Language Rights and Public Policy, Apr. 16–17, 1988 at Stanford University organized by Californians United, English Plus Information Clearinghouse, and the Joint National Committee on Languages (on file with author).

Hayakawa, S. I. 1983. English by law. *New York Times,* Sept. 30, 1983.

_____. 1985. *The English Language Amendment, one nation . . . indivisible?* Washington, DC: Washington Institute for Values in Public Policy.

Hollander, T. E. 1987. English only? Paper presented at a conference, "Language Policy in the United States," by the Global Studies Institute, Jersey City State College, Jersey City, NJ, Oct. 6, 1987 (on file with author).

Jimenez, M. 1987. Briefing paper on English-Only legislation. Mexican American Legal Defense & Educational Fund, Oct. 26, 1987 (on file with author).

Kloss, H. 1977. *The American bilingual tradition.* Rowley, MA: Newbury House Publishers.

Los Angeles Times. Immigrants—A rush to the classrooms, Sept. 24, 1986.

_____. Norman Cousins drops his support of Prop. 63, Oct. 16, 1986.

Myer v. *Nebraska,* 262 U.S. 563 (1923).

New York Times. 1986. Editorial, English yes, xenophobia no, Nov. 10, 1986.

National Education Association. 1988. Official English/English only, More than meets the eye. Washington, DC.

Pedraza, P. 1985. Language maintenance among New York Puerto Ricans. In *Spanish Language Use and Public Life in the USA,* L. E. Olivares, E. A. Leone, R. Cisneros, J. R. Gutierrez, eds. Berlin: Mouton Publishers.

Rodriguez, C. 1989. *Puerto Ricans born in U.S.A.* London: Unwin Hyman, Inc.

Rodriguez Bou, I. 1966. Americanization of schools in Puerto Rico. Adapted from "Significant factors in the development of education in Puerto Rico." in *The Status of Puerto Rico: Selected background studies prepared for the United States—Puerto Rico Commission on the Status of Puerto Rico.* Washington, DC: Government Printing Office.

Ruiz, E. 1989. The English only movement: Is it constitutional? In *Marintaya,* State University of New York at Old Westbury Newsletter of Bilingual Teacher Education Program, Spring 1989.

San Juan Cafferty, P., and C. Rivera Martinez. 1981. Bilingual education in Puerto Rico. In *The Politics of language: The dilemma of bilingual education for Puerto Ricans.* Boulder CO: Westview Press.

San Miguel, G. 1986. One country, one language: A historical sketch of English Language movements in the United States. In *Are English Language Amendments in the national interest?* Claremont, CA: Macias, Reynaldo, ed. Tomas Rivera Center

Tanton, J. 1986. Memorandum of Oct. 10, 1986 (on file with author).

Torruellas, R. 1989. Alfabetizacion de adultos en "'El Barrio'"—Distrezas basicas o educacion popular? *Centro Bulletin,* 2:6 (Summer 1989). New York: Centro de Estudios Puertorriquenos, Hunter College.

Trasvian, J. 1988. Lecture presented at the Conference on Language Rights and Public Policy. See Guy 1988.

U.S. English. Pamphlet, In defense of our common language. Undated (on file with author).

_____. Frequently used arguments against the legal protection of English. Undated (on file with author).

_____. Testimony by Luis Acle before the U.S. Senate Committee on Energy and Natural Resources on S. 712. July 14, 1989 (on file with author).

Wall Street Journal. November 1986 [quoting a Monterey County, California, Superintendent of Schools].

Wittke, C., 1939. *We who built America, The saga of the immigrant.* Western Research University Press.

Zentella, A. C. 1987. Language politics in the USA: The English only movement. Paper adapted from presentation for the Dec. 29, 1987 meeting of the Modern Language Association (on file with author).

2

Who Are the Americans?

Samuel Hernandez, Jr.

*Student, College of Staten Island,
City University of New York*

After watching the video tape shown in class about the debate on making English the only official language in the United States, I've been giving this matter a lot of thought. The part of the tape that called my attention the most was when one lady referred to Union City, New Jersey. She made the comment that when she visits Union City and sees all the Hispanic people that live there, it's like being in another country, not in America. She also mentioned that these people should only speak English if they are living here in America. At that moment, I asked myself: Who are the Americans? What do you have to do to become an American? Does speaking English or another language other than English make a person less American? In this paper I am writing and I want to express how I feel about this issue based on my personal experience.

First of all, I am from Puerto Rico. The population of the island is 3.5 million and we are American citizens. However, the national language is Spanish, not English. I served in the United States Army for four years. At the present time I am serving in the United States Coast Guard. During my military service I have been told many times not to speak Spanish, that I was in America and I have to speak English. The same phrase used by the lady on the tape.

Back in 1985 I was assigned to a Coast Guard ship. When I reported onboard at Miami, Florida, I was the only Spanish speaker on that unit. Due to the mission of the crew to patrol the Caribbean and Central and South America, they needed someone with good Spanish skills with the duties of an interpreter. So I was assigned as a Spanish-English interpreter. About 95 percent of the cases that we were involved in, such as search and rescue, law enforcement, boat safety inspections, training conducted with Latin American armed forces, visits by diplomats from these countries, etc., were conducted in Spanish.

As an interpreter, I was responsible for radio communications with persons (Spanish speakers) in distress and finding out their locations. I was a boarding officer, responsible for the communication between my ship and the owners of vessels suspected of bringing illegal aliens or drugs into the United States. After boarding these vessels and finding evidence of these violations, I was assigned to read the Miranda rights and to arrest them if necessary. I was the only one able to do this if these individuals only spoke Spanish.

I really enjoyed my job and my position as an interpreter which kept me very busy. However, during the period of time onboard the ship, I had to face other circumstances which made me angry. For instance, one day I was lifting weights on my time off. I was the only person in the weightroom of the ship and I was listening to Spanish music with a portable cassette. I was almost finished when an officer walked into the weightroom. The first thing he told me was, "How about changing the music?" With his tone of voice, it sounded more like an order than question. My answer was, "Do not worry, sir! I am leaving now and you can play your music," and I left. As an officer in the military, he could have asked me in a more polite manner. He should have set an example and not used his authority on his behalf.

Another time, I was talking on the phone in Spanish and I was told by a supervisor to speak English so everybody could understand me. First of all, the person who told me that did not know if the person I was talking to spoke English. Second, that was a private conversation and nobody had to listen to it. What makes me angry is that I was required to use my Spanish skills on a daily basis for the ship's mission and forbidden in other situations, such as listening to my music or talking on the phone. Personally I feel that I did a very important contribution to the Coast Guard and to this country, but I was not treated fairly and equally.

Presently there are many Hispanics (Puerto Ricans, Mexican-Americans, etc.) in the United States Coast Guard. There are also thousands of Hispanic Americans serving in the armed forces all over the world. The majority of American troops attached to Central America are from the U.S. National Guard of Puerto Rico, due to their Spanish skill. For many years, Hispanic Americans have fought and given their lives. Puerto Ricans, as American citizens, were drafted and sent to war during World War I, World War II, the Korean War, and the Vietnam War. Puerto Ricans were sent straight to Germany and Korea from Puerto Rico. Many of them never visited the United States or spoke any English.

For example, my father at the age of eighteen, received a letter from the U.S. Army ordering him to report for a physical exam at a military base in Puerto Rico. After he passed the physical, he was drafted into the Army. He took his basic training in that same military base without leaving Puerto Rico. After eight weeks of training he was sent to Germany with many others. I am sure that at that time nobody worried about them knowing or talking English. Two years later, after finishing his tour of duty, he was sent to New Jersey for his outprocessing and then back home. Hispanics have been serving and defending this country as any other American from the mainland. For this reason, I became very disappointed when I heard the phrase used by the lady on the tape that it is like being in another country when she referred to the Hispanic population in New Jersey.

We Hispanics have earned the right to be Americans. As a Hispanic American, I am proud of serving my country and of using my Spanish skill to benefit my country. I agree that any person who comes to the United States must make every effort to learn and develop good English skills. I do not believe that speaking other languages can lead to a division of this country like the people were saying on the videotape. For these reasons based on my personal experience, I strongly oppose the idea of making English the only official language in the United States.

3

Living in Exile
The Haitian Experience

Georges Fouron
State University of New York, Stony Brook

The contemporary re-evaluation of the world's migratory movements has produced an abundant literature on the causes and effects of migration and has inspired a growing number of researchers to look for a more comprehensive approach to this pervasive phenomenon. This new current, called the "Dependency Theory of Migration" (Portes 1979; Zolberg 1979; Sassen-Koob 1980; Cardenas 1978), portrays the movements of workers, both national and international, as the corollary of the relationship that exists between developed and underdeveloped communities and the pauperization that results from such an arrangement (Frank 1981; Walton 1976).

The Dependency Theory of Migration

The progressive transformation of capitalism into an encompassing worldwide system has brought to the fore the realities of the less developed economies by revealing their total dependency upon their richer and powerful neighbors. The dependency theorists show that contemporary world economic order is divided into two distinct and separate, yet interdependent, camps: the center or developed economies and the peripheral or underdeveloped economies. The center or developed economies are driven by an ever-ending process of profit-seeking ventures that tend *to force* the peripheral or underdeveloped economies into their sphere of influence. As a result, the underdeveloped economies become bound into a system of exchange mechanisms controlled and manipulated by the central economies, which forces the poor economies into dependency and compels them to release labor. This imported labor is very often used by the elite of the labor-importing economies to fill the bottom part of the occupational pyramid and to combat the organizational efforts of the indigenous working class (Portes 1983). These mechanisms protect the interests of the political and economic elites in both the developed and underdeveloped economies, suffocate the less developed economies, and condition them to stagnate. In the end, poor economies are transformed into mere links in the chain of a national-international exploitative system that produces internal colonialism and/or international dependency.

The consequences of the economic and political dependency that ensues are many and far reaching. Dependent economies are often deprived of their political and social sovereignty, and their cultural relevance is often ignored. Dependency also fosters and nurtures alliances between the industrial and commercial elites of both the centers and the peripheries and promotes the penetration of the political and economic institutions of the developed sector into the subordinate one. These alliances "create imbalances between sectors and institutions of the subordinate society that lead eventually to labor displacement" (Portes 1979, 427) and loss of political and economic autonomy.

Using the dependency perspective, this chapter will examine the social and economic factors that determined and influenced migration from Haiti to the United States, the immigrants' processes of adaptation, their children's experiences in American schools, and the subsequent coping mechanism used by these children and their parents to survive the uninviting living conditions offered by the host society.

Haitian Migration to the Periphery

Since the beginning of the twentieth century, American capitalist ventures in Latin America and the Caribbean region have dominated the local economies in their modalities of production and subsistence. During the early years of the twentieth century, American capitalists replaced the European entrepreneurs established in Haiti and dominated the country's economy. Among the first American corporations to take advantage of the American dominance of the Haitian economy was the Haitian American Sugar Company. Based in Wilmington, Delaware, the company was financed, controlled, and managed by American interests. It initially received from the Haitian government 24,000 acres of land that had been farmed by peasants for generations and the exclusive rights to "plant, cultivate, produce, buy, fabricate, prepare, sell and in general trade in sugarcane, coffee, cotton, cocoa, tobacco, indigo, and in sisal" (Gaillard 1981, 139). The Haitian American Development Corporation, a subsidy of the Haitian American Sugar Company, received more than 30,000 acres of land for the production of sisal. The Société Haitienne de Développement Agricole, a joint venture between the Haitian and the American governments, received more than 100,000 acres of peasants' land for the production of natural rubber (Heinl & Heinl 1978). The Haitian Exploration Company of New York received a concession for copper mining in the Terre Neuve area. The American Dye Corporation won exclusive rights for the exploitation of dye wood in the northeastern part of the country. The Reynolds Mining Corporation "acquired" 150,000 acres of land for the exclusive exploitation of bauxite ore near

Miragôane, a small town located in Haiti's southern state. The Ciment D'Haiti, a conglomerate controlled by French, Haitian, and American interests, received thousands of acres of peasants' land for the production of cement for local consumption.

In conjunction with the American industrialists' takeover of the country's dynamic sector, American banking institutions, such as the National City Bank of New York, NCB, (now Citibank), took control of the country's finances. In 1911, NCB became interested in Haiti and opened a branch in Port-au-Prince. By 1913, NCB's representative in Haiti, Roger L. Farnham, was appointed vice-president of Haiti's central bank and president of Haiti's National Railroad (Barros 1984). Farnham, the unofficial State Department representative in Haiti, kept the American government abreast of occurrences in Haiti and was influential in urging Washington to occupy the country from 1915 to 1934. NCB also obtained the exclusive right to print and issue Haiti's official money, the *gourde*. When, in 1914, the Haitian government tried to regain its right to control and regulate its currency, Farnham seized Haiti's reserve ($500,000 in gold) and shipped it to New York where it was deposited in the coffers of the NCB (Heinl & Heinl 1978). The money was finally returned to Haiti, with interest calculated at 2.5 percent, in 1919 (Healy 1976). In 1917, NCB and its ally, Speyer and Co., bought out most of the French and German financial interests in Haiti and in 1919, with the direct and active encouragement of the American State Department, became—until the late 1930's—the official bank of the country (Fouron in press).

The takeover of the Haitian economy by American capitalists and National City Bank culminated in the military occupation of the country by American troops (1915–1934), opening up the Haitian economy to unbridled exploitation and putting the country in a situation of close dependency upon the will of her powerful neighbor (Nichols 1985; Barros 1984; Luc 1976). As a consequence of the economic dependency imposed on the country by the occupation forces, Haiti became a virtual colony of the Americans. Haitian peasants were dispossessed of their land to make room for that new group of entrepreneurs born out of the alliance between the local and international bourgeois classes.

American capitalist penetration destablized the Haitian economy. The Americans contributed to the country's high level of unemployment by introducing into the Haitian economy U.S.-manufactured goods that competed unfairly against and finally replaced local products. Also the increasing need to acquire American products contributed to the country's high inflationary rates that, in the end, weakened its already dependent economy. American capitalists proposed migration as a salaried alternative to the small emerging urban proletariat and the masses of dispossessed peasants. These groups were encouraged to migrate to Cuba, the Dominican Republic, Panama, and the Bahamas where they replaced or supplemented the local indigenous labor force in industries controlled by American interests established in these peripheral economies.

The end of the American occupation (1934) did not signify an improvement in the internal conditions of the country. Sectors of the Haitian ruling strata that had collaborated with the Americans continued to rule the country and monopolized the vital sectors of the economy for their sole interest and that of the American capitalist forces that continued to shore them up. Consequently, both the Haitian bourgeoisie and its international allies failed to address the pertinent questions of progress and economic stability and neglected the real needs of the nation.

Between 1915 and 1957, mostly dispossessed and disenfranchised elements of the peasantry and the lower classes were forced to emigrate as workers to the economies of the peripheries. These movements of workers were effectuated at times legally (through government-to-government contracts) and at times illegally, but always with the implied complicity of the governments and foreign entrepreneurs involved.

Migration to the Center Economies

Migration to the United States: First Period 1957–1971

The accession to power in 1957 of François "Papa Doc" Duvalier changed the nature of the Haitian foreign migration drive. The Haitian exodus acquired three important new characteristics that profoundly transformed it. *First,* representative elements of *all* the Haitian social classes were forced to leave the country. *Second,* Haitian migration was not only directed toward the peripheral zones but also toward the center economies as well. *Third,* migration out of Haiti was openly encouraged by (1) the host societies whose representatives went to Haiti, in the 1960s, to recruit the skilled and semiskilled labor force to replenish the American working-class sector depleted by the growing need for soldiers in Vietnam; and (2) by international organizations, such as the United Nations and UNESCO, which recruited skilled labor for the newly independent African nations and the centers' cadre (Fouron 1985).

To better serve the purpose of this analysis, the Haitian migration movement to the United States will be divided into two distinct periods: from 1957–71 and 1971–89. From 1957 to 1971, Haitian immigration was primarily fueled by deep-seated fear of brutal political repression with which the Duvalier government intimidated dynamic sectors of the population that were showing signs of rebelling against its barbaric and arbitrary rule. In general, these immigrants were educated at various levels, most had emigrated with some mastery of French, were "needed" in America, and had some assets, and a great number were sufficiently familiar with the centers' mores, manners, and mentality to warrant guarded admission into America's mainstream. Most left their native land with the belief that their stay in the United States would be temporary and that it would end with the overthrow of the regime in power in Haiti. To materialize that dream, they recruited the assistance of the progressive American sectors that were opposed to the perpetuation of a dictatorial regime in Haiti. Haitian immigrants articulated their grievances adequately enough to obtain Washington's moral support in their efforts to rid the country of the Duvalier regime. Due to their persistent lobbying, President Kennedy offered them this support, treated them as political refugees, and gave them financial assistance to reach their goals. Washington's assistance, notwithstanding its moral boost, nevertheless failed to help the exiles unseat the regime and, worse yet, each failure they endured reinforced the Duvalier government's grip on the country. Even though President Kennedy's rhetoric was replete with references to "self-determination" and "democratic principles," Washington nevertheless appreciated the "political stability" that Duvalier guaranteed and the "anticommunist" stand of the regime. In the end, the Kennedy Administration restrained itself from using forceful and effective strategies to unseat the regime and finally learned to live with it. Duvalier was an SOB, but he was a pro-American and anticommunist SOB.

In the wake of Kennedy's assassination, the American government restrengthened its ties with the Haitian regime, and President Johnson openly pledged his support to the Duvalier government. President Johnson's personal investment in the Haitian economy (through Bobby Baker, a convicted swindler, Johnson had invested in a Haitian meat-packing venture, the Haitian American Meat and Provision Company, and also held substantial interests in a Haitian flour-treating plant, the Caribbean Mills) acted as deterrent to any action of the American government to unseat the Duvalier regime (Heinl & Heinl 1978; Goldman 1969).

As a result of the rapprochement between the Haitian and American governments, Haitians gradually lost hope in the ability of the "exiles" to rally the Americans on their side to destabilize the Duvalier dynasty. Subsequently, those who had remained in Haiti felt that their only alternative was to flee the country.

Migration to the United States: Second Period 1971–1989

The second period began with the death of François Duvalier in 1971 and his subsequent replacement by his son "Baby Doc" as "president for life." By that time, the international community (the Vatican, Washington, and the European nations) had made its peace with the Duvalier government. The American government's traditional foreign policy stand that preferred the "political stability" maintained by the Duvalier regime over the possibility of influencing truly democratic rule in Haiti was reaffirmed. And when, in 1969, President Nixon sent his special envoy to Haiti to show support for the Haitian regime, the Haitian people felt betrayed and lost hope in the success of their dream of democratic rule in Haiti. Nixon's special envoy, New York's Governor Nelson Rockefeller, publicly embraced a dying Duvalier on the balcony of the presidential palace in Port-au-Prince and announced that the American government would stand by the Haitian regime. That show of support won Duvalier's Machiavellian methods a decisive political victory over the opposition forces. To assure that the transition from father to son took place without a hitch, the Americans kept at bay the exiled elements who wanted to effect real change in Haiti.

The attitudes of the Americans vis-à-vis Duvalier and the Haitian population can be attributed to several factors. In conjunction with and in addition to the fact that the United States feared an imagined Cuban-like revolution in Haiti, the American business community wished to protect its substantial investments in Haiti even if it meant sacrificing the possibility of establishing a truly democratic system in that country. American foreign policy practices, which always favor stability over democratic rule, were reaffirmed, especially when that stability was being guaranteed by an authoritarian right-wing regime (Langley 1985). Moreover, American business was determined to preserve the Caribbean region as one of the most important sources of cheap and overabundant labor for its industries that were being revitalized by the war in Vietnam.

The de-escalation of the Vietnamese conflict and the imminent end of hostilities in Southeast Asia provoked a recession that had significant impact on the quality of life in the United States. The deterioration of the American standard of living, marked by galloping inflation, rising unemployment, and a general displeasure with the conditions of life in the United States, was blamed on immigrants. By the 1980s, the American government's policies were articulated from the perspectives of a new conservatism, and new strategies were adopted to stem the growing number of third world immigrants that seemed to "assault" the American labor market.

To keep at bay the surge of third world migrants, to pacify that mounting public resentment, and to offer a sacrificial lamb to cure the malaise that permeated the American economy, the United States adopted an economic policy that supported exporting nonspecialized and low-paying jobs to third world economies instead of importing cheap labor to America. The Reagan Administration initiated the Caribbean Basin Initiative (CBI) based on Sir Arthur Lewis's theory of open-door economic policies (Lewis 1955). CBI's main goal was to encourage non-growth-producing investments, such as assembly industries, in the labor-intensive sector of the dependent economies. Through CBI, generous tax incentives were extended to American firms that invested in these economies, wages were kept low to assure them maximum profit, and progressive labor laws were repealed or suppressed. In the Reagan Administration's calculation, the low-paying jobs created in these dependent economies were to act as a deterrent to the periphery-center migration movement or at the least to slow it down. But CBI's economic policies produced the reverse of what was intended. The inability of these "screwdriver industries" to absorb the large number of workers and displaced peasants looking for employment, the overcentralization of plants in the capital cities of the peripheries, and the low salaries paid the workers prevented real economic growth. As a result, the program failed to contain the migration flow. Instead, peasants and urban workers used the wages they received as the first installment on the cost of passage to a country of the periphery or to the center.

The social and economic characteristics of the second migration wave were different from those of the previous one. A large number of those who were forced to emigrate during the second period were unable to obtain visas, nor were they sponsored by other immigrants. As a consequence, they risked their lives in frail skiffs, landing on Florida's plush coastal resorts, to the discomfort and displeasure of the residents. The term "boat people," coined to describe Asians fleeing their countries at the end of the hostilities in Vietnam, was quickly applied to them. These Haitian "boat people" were stigmatized and portrayed as undesirable. They were quickly arrested, thrown into concentration camps, described as economic and not political refugees, denied lawful admission to the United States, and condemned for potentially depressing the American labor market even further.

The following section will analyze the attitudes of the Americans vis-à-vis the different migration flows, the identity imposed upon the immigrants, and their responses to these ascribed identities.

Dependency and Adaptation

Ascribed Identities

Haitians as Forming an Ethnic Group   From the inception of the Haitian migration movement to the United States in the late 1950s to the death of Duvalier in 1971, Haitians in the United States faced the difficult task of finding their niche in the host society. The first Haitian immigrants were caught in the whirlwind of ethnic pride movements that were being fueled by a revival of American ethnic consciousness. Also faced with the necessity of finding their own identity in the United States, Haitian "immigrants" (true immigrants as well as political exiles) of the first wave were schooled by the U.S. government, charitable foundations, the Democratic Party, and the inner-city educational institutions to articulate and define themselves in the host society using the rhetoric of ethnic pluralism (Glick 1972). On the economic plane, they were attracted by the Johnson Administration's efforts to implement its Great Society goals. Encouraged by the early results of the civil rights movement, and the fact that "ethnic pluralism" had become the accepted ideology for social activism in the United States (Steinberg 1981), some Haitian "leaders" began considering the possibility of organizing the immigrants as an ethnic group. These leaders also understood that ethnicity, as it complemented traditional racial patterns and replaced class characterizations, differentiated the multiple-interest groups that aspired to share in the wealth and power of American society (Glazer & Moynihan 1963). Yet Haitians had emigrated with an exalted "nationalist posture" (Trouillot 1986) centered on a vibrant and strong sense of racial pride and were unfamiliar with American ethnic considerations. In fact, racial pride was (and continues to be) so intense among the Haitians that they had appointed themselves as the legitimate redeemers of the black race. At the turn of the century, when theories of racial stratification were widespread, Haitian intellectuals wrote many books to answer the detractors of Africans, as Haitians considered themselves the standard-bearers of a race that was wrongly stigmatized. For example, Casseus's (1910) *Du Rôle Civilizateur de la Race Noire* [On the Civilizing Role of the Black Race] attacked racist European and American theorists, such as Gobineau, Chamberlain, and Hotz, and tried to demonstrate that the theory of the purported natural superiority of the white had no scientific basis. More recently the RDNP (Rassemblement des Démocrates Nationaux and Progressistes d'Haiti), the political party of the deposed president Leslie Manigat, has adopted as one of its most important political goals "the realization of fraternal equality between men [*sic*] through the *Rehabilitation of the Black race* [emphasis added]..." (Benoit 1987).

To their dismay, the immigrants were made to realize, both by their leaders and the larger American society, that in the United States resources are allocated only to those immigrant groups that can marshal their constituency into articulating their needs using an ethnic platform. Furthermore, Americans quickly identified "Haitian ethnic leaders" who showed an aptitude for articulating the needs of the "Haitian ethnic group," provided them with some financial resources, and entrusted them with the mission of convincing the Haitians to organize themselves as an "ethnic group." To drive a wedge between Haitians and native blacks and to induce the immigrants into accepting a separate ethnic identity that would, nevertheless, remain a subsection of the American black population, the larger American sector caricatured the Haitians' "French" heritage and presented them as fully Gallicized black immigrants by calling them "Frenchies" or "French Fried" (Laguerre 1984). Though tainted with ridicule, these labels were eagerly accepted by

Haitian immigrants as the probable positive mark of distinction they were searching for in American society.

While the larger American society and Haitian "leaders" were eager to create a Haitian identity that would exhibit special traits but nevertheless be included in the superordinate black ethnic sector of American society, the Haitians themselves were not sure of and unable to reach a consensus on the particular characteristics of that ethnic identity (Glick-Schiller 1975; Buchanan 1980). The efforts to organize Haitians into an ethnic group produced meager results and, in the end, Americans and their allies failed to create and implement a separate and distinct Haitian ethnic identity in the United States.

Besides the fact that the immigrants were ill-prepared to understand and master American concepts and modalities of ethnic organizing, their inability to take heed of the Americans' efforts testified to the persistence of the traditional class and color discriminatory practices they had brought with them to the United States, which continued to prevent unity and played havoc in their ranks (Paquin 1983).

Attempts to incorporate Haitians into the larger black ethnic group The waning of efforts to organize Haitians as a separate ethnic group came in the early 1970s. The federal government's contributions to promote "cultural pluralism" were severely curtailed while, concurrently, native blacks began to articulate the needs of "African-Americans" regardless of country of origin (Glick-Schiller et al. 1987). The growing political power of native blacks as it manifested itself in the visibility of the Congressional Black Caucus, created in 1971, was a force that could no longer be ignored. Haitians as well as other black immigrants were forced to see themselves as part of the general black population without any other "ethnic" considerations. Furthermore, black immigrants were informed by black American leaders that Congress was the best and most effective forum they had to present their grievances and to articulate their frustration in America.

In spite of the Black Caucus's efforts to represent all blacks as forming a homogeneous group, however, black immigrants were not convinced of the need to accept that congressional group as their advocate and did not rally en masse behind them. Contrary to what could be surmised from that attitude, the immigrants were not motivated by an antinative black posture. Their refusal to accept the leadership of the American Black Caucus was more attributable to the fact that the identity offered by black "leaders" represented an unenviable position in American society. Black identity was fine, but not when it meant incorporation and ascription in the underclass. They were avoiding being "black twice" (Glick-Schiller et al. 1987).

While the Haitians were being pressured to "melt" in the crucible of the existing black ethnic group, the "boat people" phenomenon occurred.

That phenomenon further discouraged Haitian immigrants from publicly identifying themselves as a separate and distinct Haitian ethnic group.

Frustrated by the treatment the "boat people" were receiving in America and deeply disturbed by the pervasive tendency of identifying all Haitians as "boat people," the immigrants began to shun the French label they had been so proud of a decade earlier. A great number of Haitians refused to identify themselves as such and instead used borrowed identities (West Indian, native black, Latino) to escape harassment from other ethnic groups. That attitude was so pervasive that, at the inception of the "boat people" phenomenon, American institutions engaged in the defense of refugees found it very difficult to identify Haitians willing to assist them (Glick-Schiller et al. 1987).

These negative labels did not deter *all* Haitians from identifying themselves as such and did not discourage *all* of them to come to the aid of the Haitian "boat people." Groups such as the Haitian Fathers (an exiled group of priests in Brooklyn) and the Coalition for Haitian Refugees stepped forward and initiated movements among Haitian immigrants to rescue the refugees. It was just as the efforts of these politically-organized Haitian groups engaged to help the Haitian immigrants regain their lost identities were beginning to pay off that the CDC (Centers for Disease Control), America's health watchdog, listed Haitians as a group at risk for AIDS. Immediately after the classification, Haitians were stigmatized everywhere. Leases to their apartments were not renewed, some lost their jobs, most were harassed in their neighborhoods, and their children suffered the same fate in their schools. Once more, a nefarious classification halted Haitians' efforts to situate themselves in American society and produced a chilling effect among those who were so wrongly victimized. Furthermore, the immigrants interpreted the decision of Americans to single out the Haitians as a racist ploy and an indication that life in America had come to represent a harsh exile that could be terminated only with the overthrow of the Duvalier regime in Haiti.

When Duvalier left Haiti on February 7, 1986, Haitians openly demonstrated in the main thoroughfares of the American cities they inhabited, regained pride in the Haitian identity they had temporarily abandoned, and made plans to go home to end the exile and become the true masters of their destiny. They openly rejected forced assimilation within the ranks of the native underclass, reassessed their Haitian identity based on an exalted "nationalist posture" (Trouillot 1986), and began playing a more active and open role in Haitian politics.

Chosen Identity

Transnationalism, the Final Alternative

The euphoria that was manifest among the Haitian immigrants in the wake of Duvalier's overthrow soon died down. A great number of

Haitians made the pilgrimage to Haiti and realized that realistically they could not uproot themselves to return to the homeland. Not only was the country unprepared to receive them, but, more importantly, they realized that Duvalier had left, but Duvaliérism did not go with him. Moreover, the end of the Duvalier dynasty did not signal a relaxation of U.S. control over the nation. To the contrary, the returning immigrants discovered that American capitalism had tightened its grip over the local economy and that American power, both political and economic, was expanding, not receding. In the end, they realized that true change had not taken place in Haiti. They had no alternative but to continue to live in the United States and withstand the same pressures they had tried to escape.

Faced with mounting coercive efforts of the larger society to incorporate them in the mold of the existing American underclass and with the impossibility of realizing a massive return migration movement, most Haitian immigrants have come to see their stay in the United States as a form of exile for which they have no immediate solution. While the larger American society wants to force them to accept the traditional unenviable identities of the underclass, Haitians have come to reject these identities, given the latter's precarious position in the American polity. Instead, Haitian immigrants have become *transnationalist* and use coping strategies of their own making to help them survive the negative perception the American society has of them (Basch, Glick-Schiller and Szanton in press).

Transnationalism implies that migrants can use the advantages existing in both the home and host societies to make the migration experience livable. Haitians in the United States tend to take advantage of the amenities offered by the host society, while laboring for an elusive improvement of the chaotic social, economic, and political conditions that permeate the home society, with the eventual goal of realizing the cherished dream of a return migration movement. Though that dream may be utopian, the numerous visits they make to Haiti and the active part the immigrants play in Haitian politics nevertheless help them cope with the harsh realities of their "place" in American life. These repeated contacts with the home society keep alive the possibility of an alternative solution to the unattractive options offered by American society, and palliate Haitians' fears and frustrations as immigrants in the United States.

Haitian American Identity: The Politics of Pragmatism
The painful dichotomy of living a life of exile and not being able to return home permanently mostly affects Haitians who have migrated to the United States in their adulthood. For those Haitians who were born in the United States or who migrated at an early age, America is the only social and political construct they know, and, as a result, most of them try to adapt to the modalities of the host society. They also show a ten-

dency to adopt the traits and characteristics of the communities they share with native American blacks, to the deepest chagrin of their parents. Since most Haitian immigrants are forced to live with poor blacks and have very little contact with middle-class blacks, Haitian parents tend to wrongly equate the pathologies of the ghettoes with normative American blacks' behavior patterns. This is why they are reluctant to see their children espousing "black American" ways or mores.

Haitian Immigrants and the American Schools

As blacks and inner-city dwellers, Haitian immigrants are exposed to a school system that is failing to perform its purported mission and as a result is offering second-rate education to the children entrusted to its care. Yet, coming from a society where education is the privilege of a few, Haitian parents' first and foremost concern in America is to provide a sound education for their children even though they cannot adequately articulate the latter's educational needs. They firmly believe, though naively so, that the schools exist to educate their children so that they can become productive citizens in American society. But, very often, their contact with these schools is an overpowering and traumatic experience. In most cases, Haitian parents are overwhelmed by the physical aspects of the schools and their personnel, who are mostly white. Moreover, Haitian parents do not have the knowledge to assess the problems of inner-city schools objectively nor are they aware of the proper channels for effective action. In addition, the precarious legal status of the great majority of Haitian immigrants makes them fearful not only of revealing their illegal status to the local authorities but also of seeing their children expelled from school for lack of proper immigration papers, an illegal practice that was pervasive in the 1960s. These barriers prevent them from effectively dealing with their children's numerous and complicated educational problems.

Another factor is that Haitian parents have brought with them the compliant attitude they had toward education in Haiti. In the home country, schools are often run by political cronies of the government who demand total obedience from their clientele, pupils and parents alike, lest they become impotent administrators and educators. The principal and the staff are given free reign in handling the school's affairs and must be firm, even despotic, in their dealing with parents and children alike. Haitian parents expect the same treatment from the American schools. The laissez-faire climate of many American schools, coupled with pleas for parents' participation in school affairs, are not welcomed by Haitian parents, who often interpret these attitudes as signs of weakness or disinterest.

Last but not least, the peculiar and special language predicament of the Haitian parents prevents meaningful interaction with the schools.

While the overwhelming majority of them are Creole speakers, they nevertheless present themselves for reason of prestige and survival as French speakers, thus contributing further to confusion in the communication process (Buchanan 1987).

All the preceding factors contribute to the alienation of the majority of Haitian parents from the American schools. Their participation in the activities and decision-making process is minimal at best. They rapidly lose faith in the American educational system which they condemn for being too lax and too racist.

Also, American school administrators have opted to ignore the fact that while Haitians are blacks, their particular culture and history have fostered needs that may be different from those of native blacks. American schools are teaching Haitians, a majority-oriented people, how to acquire a minority-oriented mentality. As a result, Haitian immigrants' children have come to experience a deep sense of frustration in the classroom. Verdet (1976, 232) expressed their difficulties in these terms:

> Haitian students are treated as if they were stupid, because they are slow. They can't show what they know because they don't quite understand what is asked of them. As they learn English, they forget basic arithmetic. They can't win...those Haitians who are admirable with their ESL teachers get unruly if they become the majority in an ordinary class. This obstreperousness relieves their frustration but increases that of their teachers to the point of desperation. When they are the minority, on the contrary, they suffer in silence, and one worries at the harm done their self-image by the grades and rebuffs they receive.

Conclusion

In general, Haitian immigrants are alienated from American life. They suffer from a deep sense of social and racial disorientation by refusing to conform to the ethnic ascriptions imposed by the larger American society. Consequently, for the majority of them, their lifestyle is still characterized by Haitian norms and value systems that have been restrengthened and reaffirmed to respond to American pressures toward integration into the ranks of the existing poor and oppressed "minority groups." The Haitian immigrants' interaction with American society is strongly influenced by their particular culture and their peculiar history. Their mixed African-Caribbean-French culture, their heroic past, their dire poverty, and their pessimistic attitudes vis-à-vis American society profoundly affect their realities in the host society.

Haitian immigrants thus become part of a tenuous conflict between their status as foreign-born blacks and that of American-born blacks. Such conflict is based not on racial considerations but on the processes of absorption and adaptation into the common culture and social patterns of American society. Haitian immigrants are neither totally immersed in the American ethos, nor do they consider their return to their native country a viable alternative. They are transnationalist and see their destiny as being articulated on both scenes: Haiti and the United States. In February 1989, the provisional government of Prosper Avril gave in to the immigrants' incessant pressures by creating a national office, with ministerial rank, to address the needs of Haitian immigrants. The new law gives those who have emigrated a voice in Haitian affairs by allowing them to send representatives to the Haitian Congress and to vote in Haitian elections while residing abroad.

Also, Haitian immigrants use their racial and qua-ethnic characteristics to solicit help from diverse groups ranging from labor unions, the Congressional Black Caucus, and Caribbean immigrant groups to native blacks, thus exhibiting a certain ethnic consciousness. At times, they see themselves as a segment of the indigenous black population, at other times as an invisible immigrant group, always as exploited third world people, yet every time as Haitians, thus maintaining a separate identity in American society (Fouron in press).

Moreover, the strong differences between younger and older immigrants' perceptions of American society create grave tensions in the Haitian family structure, resulting in further destabilization of primary relations in Haitian immigrant families. Haitian immigrants' unwillingness to adapt to the host society's ascribed roles reflects a combination of factors that handicap their incorporation into the mainstream of American socioeconomic life. At the same time, these immigrants are deeply affected by the dichotomous modalities of the capitalist system. While capitalism produces the factors that encourage and foster migration, immigrants are made to feel unwanted in the host society.

The painful experience of exile is brought to reality by the position of the Haitian immigrants as blacks in a staunchly class-structured society motivated by deep-seated racial and ethnic considerations. Race, ethnicity, and economic factors, as they are manipulated in American society, contribute to the exclusion of these immigrants from the mainstream of the host country. Also American education has failed to play its purported role as "integrating agent," helping immigrants find purpose and relevance in American society. Instead, Haitian immigrants are made to feel excluded from the avenues of social mobility, which in turn forces them to reject cooptative integration as a viable solution to their realities in America.

References

Barros, J. 1984. *Haiti: De 1804 à nos jours, Vol. I & II.* [Haiti: From 1804 to the present]. Paris: L'Harmattan.

Basch, L., N. Glick-Schiller, and C. Szanton. *The transnationalization of migration: New perspective on ethnicity and race.* New York: Gordon and Breach Sciences Publishers, Inc. In press.

Benoit, J. M. 1987. *Profil d'un Candidat.* [Profile of a candidate]. Caracas, Venezuela: Grupo Editorial Graphitec, C.A.

Buchanan, S. H. 1980. Scattered seeds: The meaning of the migration for Haitians in New York City. Ph.D. diss., New York University.

_____. 1987. Language and identity: Haitian in New York City. In *Caribbean life in New York City: Sociocultural dimensions,* ed. C. R. Sutton and E. M. Chaney, 202–217. New York: Center for Migration Studies.

Cardenas, G. 1978. Chicanos in the Midwest. *Journal of the Social Sciences* 7 (Fall 1978): 43–57.

Casseus, A. 1910. *Du rôle civilizateur de la race noire.* [On the civilizing role of the black race]. Paris: Louis Jeanrot.

Fouron, G. 1985. Patterns of adaptation of Haitian immigrants in New York City." Ed.D. diss., Teachers College, Columbia University.

_____. *Capitalism and migration: The Haitian case.* Durham, NC: Duke University Press. In press.

Frank, I. 1981. *Multinationales et développement.* [Multinational corporations and development]. Paris: Masson.

Gaillard, R. 1981. *Les blancs débarquent.* [The Whites Land]. Port-au-Prince: Imprimerie Le Natal.

Glazer, N. and D. P. Moynihan. 1963. *Beyond the melting pot: The Negroes, Puerto-Ricans, Jews, Italians, and Irish in New York City.* Cambridge, MA: M.I.T. Press.

Glick, N. 1972. Ethnic groups are made not born. In *Ethnic Encounters: Identities and Contexts,* ed. G. Hicks and P. Leis, 22–35. North Scituate, MA: Duxbury Press.

Glick-Schiller, N. 1975. The formation of a Haitian ethnic group. Ph.D. diss., Columbia University.

Glick-Schiller, N. J. DeWind, M. L. Brutus, C. Charles, G. Fouron, and A. Thomas. 1987. All in the same boat. In *Caribbean Life in New York City: Sociocultural Dimensions,* ed. R. S. Sutton and E. M. Chaney, 182–201. New York: Center For Migration Studies.

Goldman, E. F. 1969. *The tragedy of Lyndon Johnson.* New York: Dell Publishing Corporation.

Healy, D. 1976. *Gunboat diplomacy in the Wilson era: The U.S. Navy in Haiti, 1915–1916.* Madison, WI: The University of Wisconsin Press.

Heinl R. D., and N. G. Heinl. 1978. *Written in blood: The story of the Haitian people 1492–1971.* Boston: Houghton Mifflin Company.

Laguerre, S. M. 1984. *American odyssey: Haitians in New York.* Ithaca, NY: Cornell University Press.

Langley, D. L. 1985. *The United States and the Caribbean in the twentieth century.* Athens, GA: The University of Georgia Press.

Lewis, A. 1955. *The theory of economic growth.* London: George Allen & Unwin Ltd.

Luc, J. 1976. *Structures économiques et luttes nationales populaires en Haiti*. [Economic structures and grass-root national struggles in Haiti]. Montreal, Canada: Éditions Nouvelles Optiques.

Lundahl, M. 1979. *Peasants and poverty: A study of Haiti*. New York: St. Martin Press.

Nichols, D. 1985. *Haiti in Caribbean context: Ethnicity, economy, and revolt*. London: Macmillan.

Paquin, L. 1983. *The Haitians: Class and color politics*. New York. Privately printed.

Portes, A. 1979. Illegal immigration and the international system: Lessons from recent legal Mexican immigrants to the United States." *Social Problems* 26 (April 1979): 425–38.

_____. 1983. "Modes of Structural Incorporation and Present Theories of Labor Immigration." In *Global Trends in Migration: Theory and Research on International Population Movements,* ed. M. M. Kritz, B. C. Keely, and S. M. Tomasi, 279–97. New York: The Center for Migration Studies.

Sassen-Koob, S. 1980. Immigrants and minority workers in the organization of the labor process. *The Journal of Ethnic Studies* 8 (Spring 1980): 1–34.

Steinberg, S. 1981. *The ethnic myth: Race, ethnicity, and class in America*. Boston: Beacon Press.

Trouillot, M.-R. 1986. *Les racines historiques de l'état Duvaliérien*. [The historical foundations of the Duvalierist regime]. Port-au-Prince, Haiti: Editions Deschamps.

Verdet, P. 1976. Trying times: Haitian youth in an inner city high school. *Social Problems* 24: 228–33.

Walton, J. 1976. Urban hierarchies and patterns of dependence in Latin America: Theoretical bases for a new research agenda. In *Current Perspectives in Latin American Urban Research*. ed. A. Portes and H. L. Browning, 43–69. Austin, TX: University of Texas Press.

Zolberg, A. R. 1979. International migration policies in a changing world system. In *Human Migration: Patterns and Policies*. ed. W. H. McNeill and R. Adams, 241–86. Bloomington: Indiana University.

4

ESL and the Myth of the Model Minority

Philip Tajitsu Nash

City University of New York Law School, Queens College

Walking past the Hindi and Korean signs or stopping into stores with fragrant smells, sparkling jewelry, and colorful fabrics, visitors to the Jackson Heights section of Queens, New York, are overwhelmed by the sense of Asian/Pacific American success. Leafing through any newspaper or magazine from the local newsstand reinforces this notion with pictures of science-award winners, stories about doctors and engineers, and reports of high family income.

In the ESL classroom located on the fourth floor of a building in the heart of this bustling neighborhood, however, another side of the Asian/Pacific American experience is revealed. Here, students of all ages labor through stories, pictures, vocabulary, and grammar in order to become proficient in English. And, while some smartly-dressed, brief-case-toting professionals do show up in class, most of the students sport workday outfits of blue jeans and sneakers, indicating membership in a working class that strains behind noisy sewing machines and beneath trays of steaming food for minimum wages.

This chapter will begin with a short introduction to Asian American history, which will show how the "yellow peril" of the nineteenth century became the "model minority" of the 1970s and 1980s (Knoll 1982). Along the way, the reasons for the development of the model minority myth will be explored, using an analytical framework developed by Suzuki (1977) and built upon by Kim and Hurh (1983), Quan (1988), Kwong (1988), Osajima (1988), Nishi and Wang (1985) and others. The dichotomy between the myth and reality of today's Asian/Pacific American experience will also be explored, with attention given to how academic performance data impacts on ESL teaching. Finally, thoughts about how ESL teachers can use this knowledge to help their students will be given.

From Yellow Peril to Model Minority

Asian/Pacific Americans are relative newcomers to the United States, arriving on these shores in large numbers only after the Gold Rush in California in the late 1840s. (Cheng and Bonacich 1984). The reception accorded these new immigrants ranged, with few exceptions, from paternalism by missionaries to exploitation by labor bosses to outright lynching by mobs of labor competitors. Major events in the Asian/Pacific American experience include:

- 1790—The United States Congress limits citizenship by naturalization to free, white aliens; those of African descent become eligible for naturalization in 1870, but Asians do not.
- 1849—First large influx of Chinese laborers, many of whom come to participate in the California Gold Rush.
- 1853—California levies a Foreign Miner's Tax, which is enforced only against the Chinese; similar discriminatory laws and enforcement of laws take place in San Francisco and other localities and states.
- 1854—*People* v. *Hall* legal decision in California forbids Chinese testimony against whites in court.
- 1882—United States Congress enacts Chinese Exclusion Act to halt Chinese immigration.
- 1885—Chinese miners massacred in Rock Springs, Wyoming, and fires and vandalism hit Chinatowns in other West Coast cities; meanwhile, first large-scale immigration of Japanese takes place.
- 1894—Saito, a Japanese immigrant, applies for United States citizenship; courts refuse, because he is neither white nor of African descent.
- 1898—Annexation of Hawaii; control over the Philippines after the Spanish-American War.
- 1903—First group of one hundred Korean laborers arrives in Hawaii; meanwhile, about one thousand Japanese and Mexican sugarbeet workers hold a joint strike in Oxnard, California.
- 1906—California's 1878 statute forbidding intermarriage between whites and those of African descent is extended to include "Mongols"; these and other state antimiscegenation laws not declared unconstitutional by the United States Supreme Court until 1967.
- 1907—Japanese government protests long-time segregation of Asian/Pacific American children in public schools; President Theodore Roosevelt signs Gentlemen's agreement with Japanese government, voluntarily restricting Japanese immigration; United (Korean) Association founded in Honolulu; riots in Washington Territory force Asian Indian loggers to flee to Canada and California.
- 1913—California, followed by eight other western and midwestern states, enacts Alien Land Laws to prevent ownership of land or property by "aliens ineligible for citizenship" under the 1790 and 1870 laws; these laws not declared unconstitutional until 1948.

- 1924—Asian Exclusion Act closes door to immigration by "aliens ineligible for citizenship"; because of their colonial status as "nationals" and not "aliens," Filipinos allowed to immigrate in large numbers to fill labor shortages caused by the 1924 Act.
- 1941–42—Roundup and internment of Japanese Americans, despite high-level governmental knowledge that it was not justified by "military necessity."
- 1952—First opening of immigration from Asia, under McCarran-Walter Act.
- 1965—Amendments to the McCarran-Walter Act, including provisions to reunite families and bring in specialized workers (such as nurses, doctors, and engineers), create first large-scale immigration from Asia since 1924.
- 1975—Refugee centers open in United States and other countries for refugees from Southeast Asia; their numbers surpass 700,000 by the early 1980s.
- 1985—The Census Bureau estimates that there are five million Asian/Pacific Americans, or over 2 percent of the United States population (Knoll 1982).

One theme flowing through this sobering history of lynchings, labor segregation (we all didn't plan on running laundries), discriminatory local ordinances, racist federal laws, and other forms of discrimination is the little-recognized fact that Asian/Pacific Americans fought back. Strikes and militant labor organizing (see, for example, Ronald Takaki's *Pau Hana* for an analysis of the 1909 and 1921 sugar plantation strikes in Hawaii) were accompanied by community-financed lawsuits that resulted in rulings for equal protection (*Yick Wo* v. *Hopkins,* 1886), Citizenship (*U.S.* v. *Wong Kim Ark,* 1898) and bilingual education (*Lau* v. *Nichols,* 1974). These landmark Supreme Court cases have benefitted not only Asian/Pacific Americans but other American minorities as well.

Another example of the struggle for equal rights is the involvement by some Asian/Pacific Americans in mainstream electoral politics. They included Dalip Singh Saund, a naturalized Punjab native who represented California's Imperial and Riverside counties as a Democrat in Congress from 1956 to 1962 (Gee 1976) and Hiram Fong, a Republican Chinese American who represented Hawaii in the Senate from 1958 to 1976. Others, like Sessue Hayakawa, James Wong Howe, and Anna May Wong, chose to make their contribution to this country in the entertainment business. Most, however, were active in agriculture, fishing, logging, railroad building, small-craft industries, and family businesses.

Perceptions of Asian/Pacific Americans during the nineteenth and early twentieth centuries were stereotypical and condescending. Differences in facial features, religions, customs, dress, and language were ridiculed and vilified. As both hot and cold warfare between this country and the Philippines, Japan, North Korea, China, Vietnam, and other Asian nations developed during the twentieth century, the images of Asians and Asian/Pacific Americans in the media, textbooks, and legislative halls ranged from "Asiatic hordes" to "inscrutable J-ps" to "Yellow Peril." And, as shown by the wholesale internment of Japanese Americans during World War II and the rash of riots that pepper even the brief chronology of Asian/Pacific American history given above, the net effect of these stereotypes was often humiliating and sometimes deadly.

In 1965, however, the confluence of several global developments combined to start a refashioning of the Asian/Pacific American image. First, the failure of U.S. health-care education and science education systems to produce enough doctors, nurses, engineers, physicists, and other needed professionals led to a global search (some have called it a "brain drain") to bring young professionals and doctoral students of Asian ancestry to this country. Second, U.S. immigration laws were changed in 1965 to open the doors to family reunification and to bring in more professionals, which facilitated an Asian immigration that had been no more than a trickle since the Asian Exclusion Act closed the door in 1924; many of these professional-status immigrants went to hospitals and universities across the country, interacting in ways that working-class immigrants could not. Third, as Osajima (1988) has pointed out, articles written in the 1960s like "Success Story, Japanese-American Style" by sociologist William Peterson (*New York Times* 1966) and "Success Story of One Minority Group in the United States" (*US News and World Report,* 1966), praised Asian/Pacific Americans for using cultural strengths to overcome adversity at a time when other people of color were protesting about centuries of discrimination and injustice. The implicit message being sent to rioters in Watts and militants in El Barrio was that the system worked and that poor and undereducated peoples were responsible for their own plight. A further message, which continues to have profoundly negative effects up to the present day, was that Asian/Pacific Americans do not need help, that they were all whiz kids, and, that, if they somehow did need help, they took care of their own problems.

In a pathbreaking analysis which was published first in the *Amerasia Journal* in 1977, educator Bob H. Suzuki turned contemporary conventional thinking about the model minority on its head. Using revisionist education models developed by Bowles and Gintis (1976) and others, Suzuki rejected the notion of "cultural determinism" (i.e., Asian/Pacific Americans are just like Puritans because they subscribe to the same values of hard work, and so forth), and reminded the academic community that the model minority myth was another way of reinforcing the reproduction of an unequal class structure in American society through the social stratification of students. Suzuki's genius was found in synthesizing the visions of others into a new theory, based upon three propositions. They were the following:

1. The personality traits exhibited by Asian Americans are the result of a socialization process in which the schools play a major role through their selective reinforcement of certain cultural behavior patterns and inculcation of others that are deemed 'appropriate' for lower-echelon white-collar wage earners....

2. Although they have attained high levels of education, the upward mobility of Asian Americans has been limited by the effects of racism, and most of them have been channeled into lower-echelon white-collar jobs having little or no decision-making authority, low mobility, and low public contact, and....

3. The limited upward mobility of Asian Americans was achievable because of the demand for workers to fill lower-echelon white-collar jobs created by post-World War II expansion in the technological and bureaucratic aspects of the economy, coupled with the type of training and socialization Asian Americans had acquired through both home and extended schooling. (Suzuki 1977)

Twelve years later, Suzuki's propositions about socialization, channeling, and economic opportunity continue to hold their validity. For example, sociologists Kim and Hurh (1983) explored the model minority myth as it related to Korean American greengrocers. They found that educated elites from Korea and other countries, because they lacked English language fluency, suffered from underutilization of and unequal compensation for their educations and found themselves, temporarily at least, in the working class. Attorney Quon (1988) studied the myth as it related to lawyers and law students and found that inherent biases in the legal system, a history of discriminatory treatment, and little emotional support for would-be attorneys in the Asian/Pacific American community have stood in the way of full Asian/Pacific American participation in the legal system. Political scientist Kwong (1988), in focusing on the myth as it pertained to New York's Chinatown, found that the complex diversity of this community was usually misrepresented in the mainstream press; the steering of youngsters into science and math, but not management, continued. Finally, sociologist Nishi and social worker Wang (1985) investigated the myth in the health-care delivery system and found Asian/Pacific American health-care workers to be underpaid in relation to white colleagues with comparable education backgrounds.

Each of these studies concluded that the myth was alive and well and that it had a detrimental effect on the Asian/Pacific American community as a whole as well as Asian/Pacific Americans as individuals. And, lest anyone think that the perceived success of one immigrant might come without costs to others, including the many immigrants the successful person exploited, Kwong (1988) restates a famous Chinese saying: "For the fame of one general, ten thousand corpses are left on the battlefield."

The Asian/Pacific American Community: Facts and Consequences for ESL Teachers

It is difficult to generalize about and group into one census category people who represent over 60 percent of the world's population and a broad spectrum of languages, religions, and customs. Nevertheless, the approximately five million Americans of Asian ancestry, comprising between 2 and 3 percent of the United States population, do seem to fall into two broad categories (Hu 1989). The first, which receives much of the press coverage and which has contributed to the model minority notion, is the high education/high income group. The 1980 census found that 43 percent of Asian/Pacific Americans were in this group as managerial, professional, or service workers. While discrimination continues to haunt the high income/education group in the form of lower wages per degree earned, racially motivated slurs and physical violence, and "glass ceilings" to elite school and corporate management admissions (Hu 1989), by and large this group has the education and resource levels that will allow their children to find and make appropriate use of available ESL classes.

The second and larger group of Asian/Pacific Americans, the remaining 57 percent, is the working class—with lower education levels and lower income levels. These waiters, garment-factory workers, and small-business owners are themselves often lacking English language skills, and so their children come to ESL classes in large numbers (while Mom and Dad, if they can find time, enroll in adult education classes). This group includes most of the recent Chinese immigrants and refugees from Kampuchea (Cambodia), Vietnam, and Laos, whose especially severe problems with housing, education, and other social service needs are disguised by averaging them in with other Asian/Pacific American nationality groups.

The bipolar nature of the Asian/Pacific American population is reflected in the following statistics: In 1980, the percentage of Asian/Pacific Americans earning above $50,000 a year was 50 percent greater than for whites, while the poverty rate for Asian/Pacific Americans was, at the same time, 38 percent greater. (Hu 1989). It is also readily discernible in seemingly irreconcilable education statistics from local school districts. For example, in the 1985–86 school year, Asian/Pacific Americans made up only 6.4 percent of New York City's high school enrollment.

Yet they took a disproportionate number of seats at three elite city high schools: 24.5 percent of Brooklyn Tech, 22.3 percent of Bronx Science, and 36.5 percent of Stuyvesant (N.Y.C. Department of City Planning, 1986). Meanwhile in Boston social adjustment and economic problems have led to a disturbing increase in the Asian/Pacific American dropout rate at all grade levels since the start of the decade (Hu 1989).

On a national level, the U.S. Department of Education's Digest of Education Statistics for 1988 reminds us about the higher S.A.T. scores in mathematics, higher college enrollment rates, higher numbers of Carnegie units earned by high school students, and similarly rosy statistical tidbits about Asian/Pacific American students in the aggregate. Nevertheless, as Kwong (1988) points out, in data that others have substantiated on nationwide basis, only 28.6 percent of the "Downtown" (Chinatown-based working class) Chinese in New York possess high school diplomas and 54 percent have no English language skills, whereas the "Uptown" (foreign-born elites who get graduate training in U.S. universities) represent the top 5 percent of Chinese students allowed to go to college in Taiwan or China and were the "model" students in their native countries. Yet these elite students show up in ESL classes early in their careers and set the standard against which "Downtown" Chinese are measured.

In short, most Asian/Pacific American students in ESL classes are hampered not only by their lack of English comprehension, the lack of English-speaking parents who can help them with homework, and the lack of guidance counselors and tutors who speak their language or dialect, but also by the popular mythology that all Asian/Pacific Americans are alike and that they all are academically superior. ESL students or other students of Asian ancestry who are, for whatever reason, slow learners, are thus held up to an expectation that they cannot meet and that only exacerbates learning difficulties. These difficulties cannot be overcome simply by changing the perception of "success," but neither can each student's needs be adequately addressed until the aggregated data and popular myths give way to individual assessments of needs and strengths.

Moving Beyond the Model Minority Myth in the ESL Classroom

ESL teachers who understand the political and educational ramifications of the "model minority myth" have a responsibility to their students, and especially to their Asian/Pacific American students, to move beyond that myth in terms of classroom practices and individual interactions. What that means on a concrete level could include the following elements:

1. *Treating students as individuals and not ascribing to them good or bad characteristics or high or low expectation levels*

based on national origin or ethnicity. Kwong (1988) and others have noted that teachers and guidance counselors actively push Asian/Pacific American students into math and science disciplines, even if students are predisposed to poetry or auto mechanics. On a related note, those students from homes where both parents work long hours in service industries or who are from cultures like the Hmong (from the hills of Laos) where the language did not need to be written until the last thirty years, will have different levels of support and understanding from parents than will those students whose parents have college degrees or English language fluency.

2. *Not assuming that all Asian/Pacific American students speak the same language or dialect, or assuming that they will be friendly towards one another.* Given the history of animosities between various Asian countries, such as the forty-year occupation of Korea by Japan from 1905 to 1945, some parents harbor deep resentments against Asians of other nationalities. Also, given the current conflicts existing between Sikhs and Hindus, Vietnamese and Laotians, and others, students might have suffered physical or emotional losses at the hands of other Asians that could hinder full cooperation and interpersonal interaction with students of those backgrounds. On a related note, the written languages of China and Japan, for example, have common ideographic roots, but the Japanese language also has a simplified phonetic alphabet. Going further, the pronunciation of Chinese characters by residents of Beijing and Shanghai sound as different to them as French does to an Italian, and the question, in context, "Do you speak Chinese?" is almost as preposterous as, "Do you speak Indo-European?"

3. *Helping your school to ascertain the languages spoken by Asian/Pacific American ESL students and advocating for guidance counselors, homework tutors, and parent advocates who speak those languages.* As *New York Times* education writer Edward B. Fiske noted (March 3, 1989), the Sun Yat Sen Intermediate School 131 in New York's Chinatown helps new immigrant students do better by pairing them with "buddies" who know English and who can show them the ropes. Fiske also noted that Pace University has helped to set up at Sun Yat Sen School an after-school "Stay in School" program that offers culturally sensitive counseling and recreational activities.

4. *Taking the time to learn enough about the cultures of students to understand basic cultural differences.* For example, when most Asian youngsters avert their eyes from a teacher's glance, it is out of respect, not out of boredom or deviousness. Similarly,

as reported by the National Coalition of Advocates for Students researchers (1988), some teachers think that Asian/Pacific American students understand everything being taught in their classes when in fact their silence and smiling faces may be a cover for confusion.

5. *Not treating Asian/Pacific American students better than other students, a practice that is unfair to other students and that causes extramural animosity and violence to be directed against them.* I was involved in resolving a dispute where Euro-American teachers in a majority African American and Latino school treated the Asian/Pacific Americans as "honorary whites," thus causing racial tensions. The flip side to favoritism, which is also unfair, is excessive punishment; one Chinese American youth at an elite New York City high school was taken to court by his principal for exploding a tiny firecracker in his locker, and only intervention from Asian/Pacific American community groups resulted in a more appropriate intramural punishment.

Conclusion

The myth of the model minority has haunted Asian/Pacific Americans since the 1960s, when it replaced earlier, less positive stereotypes. While ESL teachers can help Asian/Pacific American students in their classes by understanding this myth and by working actively to treat each student as an individual, this alone is not enough. ESL teachers, with their daily contact with both the "Uptown" and "Downtown" segments of the Asian/Pacific American community, must educate the media, fellow educators, and policymakers about the true bipolar nature of the Asian/Pacific American community so that longer-term solutions to the problems of stereotyping and failing to address real needs can be formulated. As Clarence Page remarked in a *Chicago Tribune* article (1989), "In reality, the diversity that is to be found in this nation's true Asian population—as opposed to the mythical one that teams with nothing but success—offers a valuable lesson to leaders of all political persuasions: "Rather than end programs designed to help the truly disadvantaged, perhaps we need to do a better job of identifying who the truly disadvantaged are. To do that, we need a better standard than just race. We also need to look at reality."

References

Bowles, S. and H. Gintis. 1976. *Schooling in capitalist America: Educational reform and the contradictions of economic life.* New York: Basic Books.

Cheng, L., and E. Bonacich, eds. 1984. *Labor immigration under capitalism: Asian workers in the United States before World War II.* Berkeley: University of California Press.

Fiske, E. B. (1989). Meeting the needs of Asian-Americans who don't fit the "model minority" mold. *New York Times,* March 8, B8.

Gee, E. ed. 1976. *Counterpoint: Perspectives on Asian America.* Los Angeles: UCLA Asian American Studies Center.

Hu, A. 1989. Asian Americans: Model minority or double minority? *Amerasia Journal* 15: 243–57.

Kim, C., and W. M. Hurh. 1983. Korean Americans and the "success" image: A critique. *Amerasia Journal* 10: 3–21.

Knoll, T. 1982. *Becoming Americans: Asian sojourners, immigrants, and refugees in the Western United States.* Portland, OR: Coast-to-Coast Books.

Kwong, P. 1988. *The new Chinatown.* New York: Noonday Press.

New York City Department of City Planning. 1986. *Asians in New York City: A demographic summary.* December.

National Center for Education Statistics. 1988. *Digest of education statistics, 1988.* Washington, DC, USGPO, Doc. No. CS 88–600.

National Coalition of Advocates for Students (NCAS). 1988. *New voices: Immigrant students in U.S. public schools.* Boston.

Nishi, S. and C. Wang. 1985. Asian Americans in the New York State health care delivery system. *New York State Journal of Medicine,* April: 153–56.

Osajima, K. 1988. Asian Americans as the model minority: An analysis of the popular press image in the 1960s and 1980s. In *Reflections on shattered windows: Promises and prospects for Asian American studies,* ed. G. Okihiro, S. Hume, A. A. Hansen, and J. M. Lu. Pullman, WA: Washington State University Press.

Page, C. 1989. Asian Americans can't be dismissed as a "model" group. *Chicago Tribune,* April 19, p. A3.

Peterson, W. 1966. Success story, Japanese-American style. *New York Times,* Jan. 9, 20.

Quan, D. 1988. Asian Americans and the law: Fighting the myth of success. *Journal of Legal Education* 38: 619-28.

Success story of one minority group in the United States. 1966. *U.S. News and World Report,* Dec. 26.

Suzuki, B. H. 1977. Education and the socialization of Asian Americans: A revisionist analysis of the "model minority" thesis. *Amerasia Journal* 4: 23–51.

Takaki, R. 1983. Pau Hana: *Plantation life and labor in Hawaii, 1835 to 1920.* Honolulu: University of Hawaii Press.

II
EDUCATIONAL
POLICY

5

ESL on Campus
Questioning Testing and Tracking Policies

Sarah Benesch
College of Staten Island,
City University of New York

Martin R. Valdez graduated from high school in 1986 and tried to enroll in Fullerton Community College in Orange County, California. After taking the college's standardized placement test in English, Martin was excluded from college-level English and other transferable college-level courses. He did not enroll that year. In 1987 he tried again to enroll and was again excluded from college-level English and other transferable college-level courses because of his test scores. He enrolled in a remedial English course but had to withdraw because the hour conflicted with his job. Finally, he withdrew from Fullerton and enrolled in vocational training courses at a neighborhood community college.

Christopher Romero-Frias also graduated from high school in 1986. He too attempted to enroll in Fullerton Community College and, like Martin, was excluded from college-level English and other transferable college-level courses, based solely on his test scores. Christopher decided to enroll in a neighboring community college and succeeded in the same courses from which he was barred at Fullerton. However, he had to drive an extra hour and a half between home, work and, his college.

Monica Cepeda graduated from a high school in Texas in 1984 in the top 15 percent of her class. She then attended the University of Houston where she earned a 3.5 GPA after about twenty-five hours of college work. She took college-level English, psychology, and French while working forty hours a week. In November 1987, Monica moved to Fullerton, California and tried to enroll at Fullerton Community College for the winter semester in British history, world religions, and psychology. But based solely on her English test scores, she was told that she could only take a three-hour remedial English course for which she had to pay out-of-state tuition of $96 per credit. Monica found the course "elementary and demeaning."

These kinds of stories are so common that they may not shock us. We may be used to colleges excluding nonnative students from credit-bearing courses and then offering an insufficient number of noncredit courses to accommodate their work schedules. We may know students with high grade-point averages who score poorly on placement tests. And we may know students who, discouraged by their placement in elementary, noncredit courses drop out or choose to enroll in vocational programs.

The difference between the three students just described and others who may have had similar experiences is that Martin R. Valdez, Christopher Romero-Frias, and Monica Cepeda are plaintiffs in a lawsuit filed by the Mexican American Legal Defense and Education (MALDEF) on May 18, 1988, against Fullerton Community College in Orange County for its testing practices that MALDEF claims discriminate against and exclude Hispanics. The action, *Valdez* v. *Randall,* charges Fullerton with noncompliance with the Seymour-Campbell Matriculation Act of 1986, a law enacted to assess and counsel students at the community college level. The Matriculation Act provides for evaluation and placement counseling but warns against exclusionary use of the testing instruments to track students. It was enacted to ensure equal educational opportunity; MALDEF charges that it is being used to exclude Hispanic students from credit-bearing courses that are transferable to four-year schools.

The suit also accuses Fullerton of violating the due process and equal protection quarantees of Article I, section 7, of the California constitution by denying the plaintiffs access to a community college.

Valdez v. *Randall,* still unsettled at the time this book went to press, raises questions about the effects of placement testing on ESL students and curricula, and about the role of ESL education in American colleges. Do our current testing practices give us accurate information about who needs ESL instruction, and does the type of instruction offered prepare ESL students for future college work? Or do the tests and courses instead, as the plaintiffs in the MALDEF suit claim, deny these students equal access to mainstream education?

Academic Status for ESL Courses

One group concerned about the role of ESL in higher education is Teachers of English to Speakers of Other Languages (TESOL). In 1987, TESOL passed the Resolution on Granting Credit for ESL in Institutions of Higher Education, which recommended that institutions of higher education grant academic credit for ESL courses on the grounds that these courses "...demand the highest level of second language proficiency, including knowledge of contrastive phonetic, syntactic, semantic, and rhetorical information (studies that do *not* equate with remediating first language skills)..." The resolution claimed that ESL courses are as cognitively demanding as foreign language courses for which native-born students receive full credit and that they should therefore be credit-bearing.

The position that TESOL has adopted, in other words, is that ESL co instruction is both appropriate and worthy of academic status.

I too advocate full academic credit for ESL college courses. Yet I believe that ESL educators must do more than make claims about the linguistic and intellectual rigor of our courses. We must begin to examine institutional policies that may be driving our instruction, *despite our claims and best intentions,* in a remedial direction. While continuing to demonstrate the high level of academic learning that takes place in our classes, such as reading challenging texts and writing essays, we must discuss the obstacles to such learning. How can we achieve full academic membership for our students and ourselves if we ignore the impact of mechanisms such as testing and tracking that may interfere with our ability to offer full-fledged college-level instruction?

This chapter has been designed to broaden the present discussion of academic status for ESL courses. It shifts the focus from the cognitive and linguistic demands of ESL courses to testing and tracking policies that may affect the teaching and learning in the courses. To advance the idea that testing and tracking are central to academic membership, I will begin by examining statistical and anecdotal evidence about the effects of a reading test on ESL students, faculty, and curricular at one urban college. Next I will discuss a myth that seems to be the driving force behind testing and tracking, the myth of homogeneity. This is the notion that it is both possible and desirable to sort students into groups whose members have the same educational backgrounds, aspirations, and abilities. The chapter ends with examples of alternatives to testing and tracking.

Testing Reading: Effects on Students

The college where the study of testing and tracking took place uses a standardized, multiple-choice reading comprehension test of forty–forty-five questions, including main idea, direct statements, and inferences. All entering students must take the test and obtain a score above a designated cutoff to enter most mainstream classes and to graduate. Those whose scores are below the cutoff are placed in one of three reading courses for natives or one of three for nonnatives. Though these courses are not required, as they are in many colleges, most ESL students elect to take the recommended reading courses because passage of the reading test is a prerequisite to entry into many mainstream courses.

Passage and failure rates of the Fall '87 reading tests of native (NS) and nonnative (NNS) entering freshmen appear in Table 5–1. They indicate that ESL students failed the test in significantly higher percentages than did native students.

Some might argue that the percentages appearing in Table 5–1 reflect the fact that the students who failed were poor readers of English

	NS		NNS	
	pass	**fail**	**pass**	**fail**
#	679	168	40	76
%	80.1%	19.8%	54.5%	45.5%

TABLE 5–1   Passage and Failure Rates of NS and NNS on the Reading Assessment Test, Fall '87

and were therefore unready for college work. After all, it stands to res-son that a significantly higher percentage of native students would pass since they would be expected to read English more proficiently than their nonnative counterparts. Analysis of the reading test itself and the challenges it presents to nonnative students, however, call into question that interpretation of the results. Certain characteristics of the test—the emphasis on decontextualized skills (main idea, direct statements, infer-ence), possible cultural bias, and speed reading—must be taken into ac-count. Does a low score signal an inability to read college textbooks? Or does it, instead, indicate one or more of these: inability to read English quickly, confusion due to the test format, lack of experience with the background knowledge required in the inference questions? Does a passing score indicate that the student is a proficient reader and needs no additional instruction or a proficient test taker who might encounter great difficulty with a college textbook? The single score students receive on this test cannot provide answers to these questions.

One way to study the effects of testing on students is to examine the test makers' assumptions about language and learning, as revealed by the characteristics of the test. Another way is to ask students about their impressions of the test. In the following sections I will do both, be-ginning with analysis of the characteristics of the reading test.

Testing Decontextualized Skills
There is an extensive body of literature that challenges the notion of reading comprehension as a set of discrete skills (Cooper and Petrosky 1976; Smith 1982; Edelsky and Harman 1988; Valencia, Pearson, Peters, and Wixson 1989). Meaning, according to these authors, is not an object that resides in the text nor one that can be found by applying skills, such as hunting for a main idea or digging up details. It is, rather, the result of complex psycholinguistic interaction between the reader and text that includes guessing, hypothesizing, and calling upon prior knowledge. Reading, according to Valencia et al. (1989), "requires the orchestration of many reading skills" and the application of "metacognitive strategies to monitor and comprehend a variety of texts for a variety of purposes"

(58). Cooper and Petrosky (1976) shun the work *skills* altogether, preferring the term *strategies,* whose connotation is less mechanical, to describe what fluent readers do. Some of the strategies they have observed are risking errors, expecting the text to make sense, and using orthographic, syntactic, and semantic redundancies.

Edelsky and Harman (1988) have challenged test-makers' premise that reading proficiency can be measured by testing decontextualized skills that may be part of the reading process but do not individually reflect its complexity. They point out that what students are asked to do on standardized reading tests — read "pseudotexts" written by test developers and answer the questions written about those texts— is a very different activity from reading authentic texts for authentic purposes.

Testimony from ESL students reveals how reading can be distorted when it is reduced to a restricted set of skills. Here's what one student wrote about practicing for the reading test during three semesters of ESL classes:

> All teachers who were teaching me during the three semesters told us about the test. We had to read as fast as we could, so that we wouldn't spend time which is important. In addition we were advised to read while to infer the main ideas. [Ilyas, Morocco, one year in U.S.]

Ilyas had had three semesters of reading class in which his teachers, along with offering reading instruction, trained the students to distinguish three types of questions that they would find on the reading test: main idea, inference, and detail. We can see from Ilyas' account that even after this amount of training in the three skills, he still confuses the terms. This confusion is made evident by the phrase, "...to infer the main ideas." Yet Ilyas had demonstrated in his ESL reading classes that he read English well; he offered intelligent and sophisticated oral and written interpretations of such assigned works as Arthur Miller's *A View from the Bridge* and James Joyce's *Eveline.*

Other students who had failed the reading test also showed in class discussions and written work that they understood assigned works of fiction and nonfiction. An excerpt from one student's journal about the essay, "Halfway to Dick and Jane: A Puerto Rican Pilgrimage" by Jack Agueros, seems to demonstrate that she orchestrated many reading strategies, including those that are isolated on the reading test she failed: finding *the* main idea (she found more than one), remembering details, and making inferences. The unedited sample from her journal follows:

> He was loved by his parents very much. They put their hopes on him, not for them, for himself and many poor people. The parents are the people who were discriminated in American society as later he knows. His parents gave him everything: however since they

were poor, all of them are books and hand-made bookcase, which were good for his future, and the "warm atmosphere" which seemed very hard to keep in the situation at that time. Actually it is almost impossible to hide the dark side of living from curious children. However, his mother did it almost perfectly except one thing. He didn't write how he was thankful to his mother, but the emotion is felt through the whole happy memory of his childhood.

As far as this student is concerned, the main ideas of the essay are that the author's parents loved him and that they sacrificed for his future. The details she notes are the books and handmade bookcase they gave him. She infers from her reading that the author's parents tried "to hide the dark side of life" from him and that he was thankful to his mother though he did not write about his gratitude directly. This is a single sample from one student. Still, it shows that when students read captivating texts with pleasure, they may perform better as readers than when they read "pseudotexts" and try to figure out which main ideas, details, and inferences the test maker has decided to highlight.

One of the challenges for ESL students in reading classes is to reconceptualize reading to prepare for standardized tests. When they read for pleasure or to learn, they orchestrate a variety of cognitive, linguistic, affective, and metacognitive strategies, as demonstrated in the preceding example. When they read and answer questions for the reading test, they must focus on one of three isolated skills. In reducing reading to these three decontextualized skills, test makers seem to have made reading more taxing.

Testing Cultural Awareness

When taking reading comprehension tests, students must try to think like those who write the passages, questions, distractors, and answers. Owen (1985) claims in his critique of the SAT, a multiple-choice standardized test, that determining the answer is a subjective process dependent on the test taker having the same belief system as the test maker:

> There is nothing genuinely objective about a test like the SAT: it is written, compiled, keyed, and interpreted by highly subjective human beings. The principal difference between it and a test that can't be graded by a machine is that it leaves no room for more then one correct answer. It leaves no room, in other words, for people who don't see eye to eye with ETS [Educational Testing Service] (33).

Do ESL students fare worse than their native counterparts on so-called objective reading tests because they do not operate according to the same cultural assumptions as the test makers? Carrell and Eisterhold (1983), concluding a report of studies on the effects of cultural background on ESL students' reading comprehension, advise ESL' educators to be aware of the text's "social-cultural meaning, culture-specific values, and covert information" (565). And the authors remind us that lack of comprehension of a text may be attributed to "problems related to the absence of appropriate generalized information assumed by the writer and possessed by a reader sharing that writer's cultural knowledge." Yet scores on a standardized multiple-choice reading comprehension test are unable to distinguish problems with lexical items, with grammatical structure, and with cultural knowledge. Results from this type of test cannot tell us whether the nonnative test takers need additional reading instruction or whether they simply need greater exposure to the culture.

ESL students in the current study reported that eliminating distractors was difficult, especially for inference questions, because as one student put it, "Every choice looked like the answer." It may be that performing well on this test depends in part on greater experience in the target culture, experience that must be called upon while reading one short text after the other. This summoning of background knowledge is what Carrell and Eisterhold and other schema theorists call "activation of appropriate schema." If ESL students come from countries whose cultural references and knowledge are different from those of American test makers, should we not expect these students to have difficulty eliminating distractors and choosing the answer? Inference questions, for example, often require the test taker to sense that the passage has an ironic point of view and that the correct choice is therefore *not* the literal one. Is this type of distinction one that ESL students should be expected to make as they enter college? And if they cannot, should they be kept out of mainstream business and computer science classes? Research is required on the degree of cultural knowledge required to pass such tests.

Testing Speed of Reading and Extending the Gate-keeping Function of the Test

While the pedagogical, linguistic, and cultural assumptions of test makers pose difficulties for ESL students, speed is the most apparent stumbling block. This is perhaps not surprising when taking into account the difficulty of reading quickly in a second language. One might ask why speed is a component of a college reading test, especially when we consider that ESL students enrolled in college courses are often willing to read assigned material repeatedly until they master it. Students in this study reported that lack of time was a major stumbling block:

> The thirty minutes that I had for the reading test, I spend very hard to read carefully without making any error. I was nervise. I think that I know that I have to pass this reading test to get into any 200 level classes. (Kamala, Sri Lanka, three years in US.)

Kamala raises two issues here: the difficulty of reading fifteen passages and answering forty or forty-five questions in thirty minutes in his second language, and the gate-keeping function of the test. The reading test is used both as a placement instrument and, more recently, as a gate to 200-level courses (second semester or sophomore year). Before 1987, students had been able to enroll concurrently in ESL and academic courses, as long as they passed the reading test before their sixty-first credit. In 1987, the faculty voted to extend the gate-keeping function. Students must now pass the reading test in order to enroll in any 200-level course. Those voting for the new regulation were concerned that many students seemed less involved in reading textbooks, answering essay exams, and speaking up in class to ask questions or participate in discussions. They voted to bar students from 200-level classes, on the assumption that scores on a reading test would sort those who can do college work from those who cannot. Faculty members have legitimate concerns about the lack of participation of some students. However, the new regulation does not address the problem of how to increase student interest in and commitment to coursework. Rather, it drives students into remedial reading courses in which much of the time is devoted to passing the test. A vicious cycle.

A Korean student now in his senior year at the college was dismayed when the new regulation was passed. He agreed to write about his experience as a freshman taking 200-level classes before he had passed the reading test. He feels that ESL students are now being unfairly excluded from courses in which they might perform well. Incidentally, this student maintained a high grade-point average and was recently accepted at several medical schools. A portion of his unedited text follows:

> When I started college in Fall 1985, I had no English. Of course, I couldn't pass English assessment test in both reading and writing. But I took calculus I (Math 231) at my first semester. Even though I had a lot of trouble with English, Math 231 wasn't hard course for me. Actually, it was the easiest course at that semester. I had to use my dictionary when I tried to solve math problems. But after few weeks, I didn't need my dictionary at my Math 231 because I had memorized many math words and soon I found that there weren't anymore new words to memorize. The study was getting easier because the more I spent time to study the more I felt comfortable with English in it. I had no trouble to get A in Math 231....

With the new regulation, students will not have the opportunity that this student had to learn English in the rich, meaningful context of a challenging curriculum. Instead, they will take a series of ESL reading courses unrelated to their academic interests. A more pedagogically sound solution would be to provide language instruction linked directly to other academic courses. A fuller description of this type of instruction appears in the last section of the chapter and also in Chapter 9, "A Collaborative Model for Empowering Nontraditional Students."

Effects of Testing on the ESL Curriculum

Students are placed into ESL reading and writing courses solely on the basis of their test scores.[1] Results on the reading test are computed by adding up a student's correct answers. ESL students receiving a score of 19 or below on the reading test are tracked into a no-credit reading class. If their score is 19 or 20, they are tracked into a one-credit class, and if it is above 20, they go into a two-credit course. That is, choosing one incorrect answer can result in placement in a no-credit ESL reading class.

ESL faculty report that their greatest problem is reconciling language instruction with test preparation. The students, who must retake and pass the reading and writing assessment tests in order to take freshman composition and 200-level courses, understandably want to practice for the tests. Instructors, highly trained professionals, are eager to teach reading and writing, but they are compelled to help their students prepare for tests. Rather than spending a whole semester on work that might help their students in future courses, reading, discussing, and writing about whole texts, instructors must interrupt language study to focus on test taking. On the average, as much as one-quarter of the semester is devoted to aspects of test preparation, such as practicing isolated skills, eliminating distractors, speed reading, and managing anxiety. ESL faculty use humor to show the contradictions between real reading and writing and performance on the tests, but they are disturbed by the intrusion of the tests on students' learning and by the imposition of test makers' conceptions of reading and writing on the curriculum. Teaching to tests reduces their sense of professionalism.

These types of constraints have not been addressed in the literature on granting academic credit for ESL courses. Yet they figure prominently in the lives of ESL students and faculty. We in the profession have understandably been busy demonstrating that learning English as a second language is linguistically and cognitively demanding and that teaching ESL is a professional undertaking that requires training in second language acquisition, linguistics, applied linguistics, anthropology, and psychology. It is time to acknowledge to ourselves and others that as long as there are tests and tracks that keep our students out of the mainstream, they will continue to be seen as members of a remedial population and we as remedial instructors.

Myth of Homogeneity

The types of testing and tracking described above grow partly out of the myth of homogeneity, which is based on a set of assumptions about teaching and learning. One of these assumptions is that it is possible to accurately group students into homogeneous classes. Another is that students learn best when grouped with peers having similar measured abilities. The myth prevails because of the existence of standardized tests whose developers claim can sort students into groups by similar ability and knowledge. As we have seen in the discussion of one reading test,. the demands of the test itself—speed reading, controlling anxiety, eliminating distractors, depending on cultural knowledge—are also being measured, and therefore scores received may reveal as much about test-taking ability and cultural background as they do about language proficiency or future performance. This confusion is reflected in the fact that even with all the testing and tracking that goes on, homogeneity has not been achieved. In each ESL class at the college where the study took place, there are some students with greater experience in English than others; some participate and learn with more enthusiasm and ease than others. Yet the myth of homogeneity is deeply embedded in conventional wisdom. Calls for more sophisticated tests to create finer distinctions between students and for an even greater number of course levels are heard more often than calls for a questioning of the myth of homogeneity or for a reconsideration of present testing and tracking practices.

The basic premise of the myth of homogeneity, that ability grouping provides the best conditions for teaching and learning, has been challenged by Oakes (1985). After analyzing sixty years of research on tracking, she concluded that benefits for students in both low and high tracks have not been demonstrated:

> The net result of all these studies of the relationship of tracking and academic outcomes for students is a conclusion contrary to the widely held assumption about it. We can be fairly confident that bright students are *not* held back when they are in mixed classrooms. And we can be quite certain that the deficiencies of slower students are *not* more easily remediated when they are grouped together (7–8).

In her own study of tracking in twenty-five American high schools, Oakes (1986) found that students in the bottom tracks received inferior skills-based education and that placement in these tracks led to lowered self-esteem and aspirations. While students in the upper track of English had what Oakes calls "high status" curriculum, reading literature, writing essays, and doing research, students in the bottom track filled in workbooks and studied language mechanics (63). Tracking in these twenty-five schools served to widen rather than narrow gaps between high and low scoring students.

Even more surprising is Oakes' finding that high-track students did not appear to do consistently better in homogeneous groups and that in seventy-three heterogeneous English and math classes studied: "...everyone usually seems to do at least as well (and low and average students usually do better) when placed in mixed groups" (Oakes 1985, 194). Oakes concludes: "The brightest and highest achieving students do well regardless of the groups they learn with" (194).

Though Oakes did not study nonnative students as an isolated population, she did find that minority students were disproportionately represented in the bottom tracks (Oakes, 1985). Considering that the gap between those at the bottom and those at the top seems to widen due to the disparity in the types of instruction received, it is time to rethink the way we educate our immigrant students. By tracking ESL students into remedial noncredit courses, we may be penalizing them for their lack of prior experience with certain types of instruction, as the TESOL Resolution on Granting Credit for ESL in Institutions of Higher Education points out. Rather than simply asking for credit for these courses, however, we must call for a moratorium on tests that treat language as a set of decontextualized skills. And we must question the validity of a hierarchy that separates students into levels according to test scores whose meaning is indeterminate.

Alternatives to Testing and Tracking

In light of the fact that ESL programs at many colleges are so profoundly affected by testing practices, I have tried to imagine a program that was not test-driven. What would happen if there were no longer placement tests to track students and gates to keep them out of college courses? How would colleges decide which students needed additional language instruction and what type of instruction would be appropriate? How could we improve our practices so that we avoided using standardized tests to track students into various courses whose goal is, in part, to perform better on these tests? The alternative I propose is in two parts. The first deals with how to determine entering students' proficiency, the second with providing instruction that recognizes the academic rigor of both language and content teaching and respects their mutuality.

Diagnostic Interview

Suppose that instead of requiring students to take timed language tests as they entered college, we had them meet with a counselor or faculty member to work out a mutually agreed-upon program based on high school performance and future goals. The interview could include an informal screening device, such as reading and writing about a short text. This face-to-face approach is quite different from mass testing and tracking. Under circumstances in which students are given no choice or personal attention, the resentment at being placed in an ESL course, even when the student might need this type of instruction, is palpable, as many ESL instructors report.

Informal diagnostic interviewing went on in the college where the study took place before there was mass standardized language testing and the attendant proliferation of remedial and ESL writing and reading courses. There was one optional basic English course for students who, along with their counselor or advisor, decided that they could benefit from further language instruction prior to freshman composition. The course was taught by full-time faculty members who assigned plenty of reading and writing and experimented with nontraditional instruction, such as collaborative learning, that was appropriate for heterogeneous classes. Mass testing created a need for multiple levels of this basic English class to correspond to the spectrum of test scores. In other words, the purpose and structure of this single language course was transformed by the imposition of standardized tests.

Professors in the English department who placed students during the pretesting period recall that many students chose to enroll in the basic English course and seemed to appreciate the opportunity to work further on their writing and reading when given the chance to talk it over. It may be that when there were no testing and tracking mechanisms, the course was accepted as an aid rather than a punishment. According to one professor, the process was somewhat inefficient because computer printouts of students' high school transcripts were not available. He believes, though, that with the present computerization of student records, the interview system would be more effective.

Linking Content and Language Instruction

What if the diagnostic interview revealed a need for additional language instruction? Rather than enrolling the student in the noncredit, skills-based language course unrelated to other courses, the counselor could recommend a credit-bearing reading or writing course linked to a content course. This approach acknowledges that language courses are as important as other offerings. It posits language instruction as a corequisite of, not a prerequisite to, college work.

The models described below are founded on the assumption that language and content instruction are interrelated, that concepts and problems in psychology, computer science, business and other fields cannot be studied without reading, taking notes, asking questions, and other language processes. The models are also based on the assumption that students need to write about *something* in language courses. The relationship between language and other academic areas was the focus of the pioneers of the Writing across the Curriculum movement in the U.K. (Britton, Burgess, Martin, McLeod, & Rosen, 1975) and those who have kept it going in American colleges and universities (Fulwiler and Young, 1982, 1990). The following models provide alternatives to excluding students from challenging courses because of their inexperience with college material. They make it possible to use students' need for academic experience as the starting point of instruction rather than the rationale for gates. Following are some examples of linked content and language instruction:

1. Assigning trained tutors or ESL faculty to attend large lecture classes and then meet with small groups of ESL students to work on the content of the lectures through extensive speaking and writing. In this model, the content and structure of the lecture class is unchanged: the tutor-led groups use the course material as the basis for instruction, with the purpose of demystifying the language of the lectures and textbooks. Students are encouraged to share and extend their understanding of course material through informal and formal talk and writing (Hirsch 1988; Guyer and Peterson 1988).

2. Linking content and ESL courses and providing release time for faculty development and weekly meetings between content and language faculty whose courses are linked (Snow and Brinton 1989; Benesch 1988). This model centers on collaboration across the disciplines. The curriculum is developed by the content and language teachers. In the language class, students discuss, read, and write about material presented in the content course (offerings include introductory sections of psychology, computer science, business, and biology). In the content course, they listen to lectures, but they are also invited to participate more actively than students in a traditional introductory course. They ask questions, suggest topics for discussion, and participate in small group research projects.

3. Providing individualized help at writing centers where tutors have been trained to work with ESL students on reading and writing assignments from content courses.

4. A combination of the first, second, and third models in which content and language are linked, tutors attend the content classes and lead small group discussions, and one-to-one instruction in reading and writing is available at the writing center. This comprehensive model has been developed by Johns (1989) at San Diego State and Haas, Smoke, and Hernandez, (Chapter 9, this book) at Hunter College.

Conclusion

I am writing this conclusion during the last month of the semester. My students are now practicing for the upcoming reading test. We have devoted ourselves completely to this task. We are no longer reading and discussing texts about American history and culture nor writing journals and essays. The class has lost its intellectual and academic vigor. Uncharacteristically, the students are bored and withdrawn. They ask if they can leave class early even though they want to be prepared for the test. I insist that we complete the practice tests and go over the difference between main idea, detail, and inference questions. I am bored too. But to help the students pass the test, their ticket to mainstream college life, I give practice tests, time their reading, and go over answers. We discuss test-taking strategies, such as experimenting with reading the questions first, reading first those passages whose subject matter is familiar, and filling in the blank circles as the time runs out. Is this the kind of linguistically and cognitively sophisticated ESL teaching we in the field have been aspiring to and touting?

ESL educators have argued against the no-credit, nonacademic status of ESL courses. Yet we have been silent about the use of testing to exclude students from the mainstream, to justify the proliferation of levels of ESL, and to limit the intellectual life of nonmainsteam classes. This silence has permitted test makers to continue producing instruments that do not reflect important gains made over the last twenty years in understanding reading and writing processes of native and nonnative students. We know now, for example, that reading is a complex interactive process between reader and text and that writing is a recursive process of reading, writing, thinking, rewriting, seeking and using feedback, and editing. Yet widely used tests are based on simplistic notions of reading such as the application of two or three skills and writing as a matter of composing a single draft in one of three rhetorical modes.

Our silence has permitted colleges to turn ESL education into a remedial industry that relies on cheap labor (part-time instructors), and a steady supply of customers (those who fail entrance tests). In the college where the study took place, there was one basic English class before the advent of mass testing. Now there are ten, four for natives, six for nonnatives. Are the distinctions made by the tests to track students into these levels meaningful? Why are the classes still heterogeneous? What are the differences in the way low-tracked and high-tracked ESL students are taught? What would be the benefits of offering several sections, each linked to a different content course, of a credit-bearing ESL course that took heterogeneity into account?

Our silence has allowed testing and tracking to affect the quality of our teaching. While we know that genuine reading and writing are different from the activities required to pass tests, we are obliged to instruct our students in an unprofessional manner so that they can pass through gates. First we assist them to become better readers and writers and then we ask them to set aside the newly-learned strategies and practice test makers' reductive version of reading and writing—language as decontexturalized skills within a predetermined time frame. It is important to reiterate here that it is not enough to claim that our courses are worthy of academic credit. We must ensure that they are in no way remedial by rejecting policies that lower the intellectual level of our teaching. Perhaps *Valdez* v. *Randall* will be an important precedent in abolishing the exclusionary use of testing and dismantling tracking. In the meantime, ESL faculty and students can continue as advocates for academic membership by examining and challenging the tests used to track ESL students. We can also demonstrate to colleagues and administrators that ESL instruction is not remedial and that language and content courses are equally demanding and mutually beneficial.

References

Benesch, S. 1988. Linking content and language teachers: Collaboration across the curriculum. In *Ending remediation: linking ESL and content in higher education,* ed. S. Benesch.

Britton, J., T. Burgess, N. Martin, A. McLeod, and H. Rosen, 1975. *The development of writing abilities,* (11–18) London: Macmillan Education.

Carrell, P. L., and J. C. Eisterhold. Schema theory and ESL reading pedagogy. *TESOL Quarterly,* 17(4): 553–73.

Cooper, C., and A. Petrosky, 1976. A psycholinguistic view of the fluent reading process. *Journal of Reading* 20(3): 184–207.

Edelsky, C., and S. Harman, 1988. One more critique of reading tests with two differences. *English Education,* 20 (3): 157–71.

Fulwiler, T., and A. Young, 1982. *Language connections: Reading and writing across the curriculum.* Urbana, IL: National Council of Teachers of English.

_____. 1990. *Programs that work: Models and methods for writing across the curriculum.* Portsmouth, NH: Boynton/Cook.

Guyer, E. and P. W. Peterson, 1988. Language and/or content? Principles and procedures for materials development in an adjunct course. In *Ending remediation: Linking ESL and content in higher education,* ed. S. Benesch. Washington, DC: TESOL.

Hirsch, L., 1988. Language across the curriculum: A model for ESL students in content courses. In *Ending remediation: Linking ESL and content in higher education,* ed. S. Benesch. Washington, DC: TESOL.

Johns, A., 1989. EAP course design and the issue of transferable skills. Paper presented at the 23rd annual TESOL convention, San Antonio, TX.

Oakes, J., 1985. *Keeping track: How schools structure inequality.* New Haven: Yale University Press.

Oakes, J., 1986. Tracking, inequality, and the rhetoric of reform: Why schools don't change. *Journal of Education* 168 (1): 60–80.

Owen, D., 1985. *None of the above: Behind the myth of scholastic aptitude.* Boston: Houghton Mifflin.

Smith, F., 1983. *Essays into literacy*. Portsmouth, NH: Heinemann.

Snow, M. A., and D. M. Brinton, 1988. Content-based language instruction: Investigating the effectiveness of the adjunct model. *TESOL Quarterly* 22 (4): 553–74.

Valencia, S. W., P. D. Pearson, C. W. Peters, and K. K. Wixson, 1989. Theory and practice in statewide reading assessment: Closing the gap. *Educational Leadership,* 46 (7): 57–63.

1. The writing test is a fifty-minute holistically-scored argumentative essay. Students must pass this test to qualify for freshman composition, a prerequisite to many college courses. While it would be possible to study the writing test using similar questions about speed and cultural awareness, I have chosen to concentrate on the reading test.

6

Contextual Complexities
Written Language Policies
for Bilingual Programs

Carole Edelsky and Sarah Hudelson
Arizona State University

Introduction

Imagine this situation. You are interviewing for the position of director of bilingual/second language education in an urban school district of almost 100,000 students. Until twenty years ago, the district's student population was 85 percent Caucasian and 15 percent Black, with a few Mexican American migrant children. Since that time, immigration has resulted in an influx of students from a variety of ethnic and language backgrounds. The largest population of non-English speakers, about 10,000 in number, is Hispanic. The earliest Hispanic immigrants were of Cuban origin, followed by Venezuelans and Colombians, but now most of the Spanish speakers entering the school district come from war-torn Central America. Most of the first waves of Spanish-speaking immigrant children came from well-educated middle class families. Many of the more recent immigrants have not been to school or have had their schooling interrupted by war.

The next populous group of immigrants (about one thousand students) are of Haitian origin. The home language is Haitian Creole. The majority of the Haitian students enrolled in this school system have not been to school in their own country. The few who did go to school in Haiti were in schools conducted in French, a language the children did not use in their homes. Only after the Duvaliers were overthrown in 1986 did Haiti award Haitian Creole official language status along with French. And only in the last five years has any Haitian Creole been permitted to be a medium of instruction.

Another smaller group of immigrants are Southeast Asian refugees from Vietnam, Thailand, and Laos. The educational backgrounds (as well as the languages) of these five hundred students vary. Most of the more recent arrivals have spent considerable time in refugee camps waiting to come to this country. In these camps schooling focused on teaching English.

Reprinted with permission from *Center for the Study of Writing Technical Report/Occasional Paper Series*, 10, June 1989.

There is also a group of about one hundred Russian speakers in the schools, since this district is one of the official ports of entry for Russian Jewish immigrants. In addition to these non-English speakers, there are small numbers of students from more than eighty other language groups, including Arabic, Chinese, French, and Portuguese.

Student populations vary tremendously from school to school. Some schools are almost 100 percent Hispanic or American Black and Haitian. Others are almost exclusively white non-Hispanic with a few non-English speakers from different native language backgrounds. And there is every possible combination between those two extremes.

One of the questions posed during the interview is the following: Given the situation just described, what kind of a design would you propose for bilingual and/or second language instruction in the school district? More specifically, what would you propose in terms of the language or languages used for non-English-speaking students' writing and reading instruction?

From our perspective, the "ideal" or theoretically preferred answer would be that students' native languages would be used in written language instruction, that students would have an opportunity to develop first as readers and writers in their home languages and then gradually add on English literacy. We base our ideal answer on (1) the theoretical stance, articulated by UNESCO (1953), for initial literacy in the vernacular followed by second language literacy; (2) research evidence demonstrating that quality bilingual education programs benefit children in terms of both their academic and English language achievement (General Accounting Office, 1987; Hakuta 1986; Rosier and Holm; Troike 1979) and on our own work in bilingual education (see for example, Edelsky 1986; Hudelson 1987).

But while there may be a theoretically "correct" answer, the educational and noneducational realities that individual communities face—conditions permitting (or not)—make it impossible to offer one policy regarding written language instruction that will be appropriate for all educational scenes. Therefore, instead of offering a single policy, we will present a general position. Then we will argue against national or state-level policies that are highly specified by pointing out just a few of the complex variations that can exist between any two bilingual programs. We follow this discussion by elaborating some of the issues that must be considered by those making local decisions so that their schools can be guided by sensitive, informed policies that work well in their own localities.

Our position is this: For teaching and learning written language use, teachers and students must have autonomy and must be able to appropriately account for local conditions. Therefore, upper level governmental policies should be broad, nonspecific, and linked to appropriate *general* goals. Local program policies should be developed locally to consider (but not always acquiesce to) the details of the local situation while still leaving responsibility for major decisions to individual teachers. We take this position because learning to write in school (whether or not in a school with a bilingual program) always happens in multiple co-occurring contexts; because each of those contexts has profound effects on the learning and teaching of writing inside the classroom (see Edelsky 1986 for a discussion of one case); and because the contexts are complex in ways that may not be immediately obvious.

Contextual Variation Precluding Uniform Policies

The Languages Involved

Writing occurs during time and group arrangements within classrooms within schools within communities within school districts within large geographic and political regions that exist at certain historical times and are brought to life by people with varying interests and beliefs. Although larger contexts influence smaller and vice versa and although the smaller contexts are tied together at least through their membership in the same gigantic political-economic-social-historical context (e.g., the United States in 1990), these smaller contexts present a dizzying variety of details.

In the United States, the "other" school language, which Fishman (1976) calls the marked language, may not be the student's home language (e.g., the students may speak nonstandard Puerto Rican Spanish and be placed in a Standard Mexican Spanish bilingual program in Chicago). If the non-English school language *is* the student's home language, it is not simply an uncomplicated "other." Students may come to school speaking a standardized dialect of a world language (e.g., Standard Mexico City Spanish), a nonstandardized dialect of a world language (e.g., a nonstandard working class dialect of Mexican Spanish), a standardized dialect of a regional written language (e.g., Standard Vietnamese), a nonstandardized dialect of a regional language with a long written tradition (e.g., certain dialects of chinese), or a regional language without a long written tradition (e.g., Hopi or Haitian Creole). Furthermore, there are many possibilities for what varieties of English are used in the students' communities.

Teachers' Bilinguality and Biliteracy

Describing the bilinguality of teachers in a bilingual program may also be complicated. Teachers themselves may have gone to school and been educated as professionals in the students' home language and then received more professional education in the second language. Thus they may be more literate in the home language than in English, as well as more familiar with oral school registers in the home language (e.g.,

Cuban teachers in Miami). Or, teachers may share the students' home language but have no school experience with it, having been educated only in their second language. These teachers would be considerably more literate in their second language than in their first (e.g., some Chicano teachers in the Southwest, many Haitian teachers educated in French in Haiti). Or teachers may have attended lower grades in the students' home language and then received higher levels of schooling and all professional education in the second language (e.g., teachers who immigrated to the United States in their teens).

Language Use in the Community

Outside the classroom, the bilingual-program students' community is not one that simply uses language X plus English or just language X. In each community, there will be differences in where and how English and the other language are used. In some places, there may be clear boundaries for the use of one language or the other, with business and government requiring English and home and religion the other language. In other communities, it may be acceptable to use each language in all settings, but variation within the setting (who is speaking, who is listening, who is listening in, what purposes the language is being used for, how formal or informal the particular moment is) demands a shift from one language to the other (Grosjean 1982).

Pressure from the "Larger" Context

Other outside contexts—not so nearby as the immediate neighborhood— contribute their own complicating factors to how writing occurs in particular classrooms. What complicates here is not the tremendous variety, but the potential for tremendous and often deleterious impact. These more distant, more abstract contexts, which might account for state and regional "climates," national "temper of the times," and prevailing values, become more concrete through school district policies, state legislative and state department policies and mandates, federal statutes, federal agency policies and recommendations, and state and federal court decisions.

Testing, for example, is a central fact to be dealt with in every classroom in the United States. The power of a school's testing program to influence writing instruction comes from contexts outside the school itself. The general public's faith in tests and testing as valid indicators of learning, educational excellence, teaching, etc. (see Edelsky and Harman 1988 and Meier 1981 for critiques of tests), the reliance on test data in recent national reports on the state of education, the increased numbers of state-required tests for increased numbers of children, and the growing practice of publishing test scores in local newspapers put much pressure on the teacher and children in any particular classroom. When tests are so central, the language of the tests (usually English) becomes the "real" or important language of the classroom; the tasks demanded by the tests become the "real" tasks, and the way test language is conceptualized (as consisting of small separable components with an emphasis on the most easily measured) becomes the "real" way to think about language.

Mandated tests are tied to other moves in the larger contexts—moves for standardization and control over teachers. One example is pressure for a standard curriculum with a district-established scope and sequence for district-specified objectives. Like standardized tests, small objectives and scope-and-sequence charts emphasize low-level conventions. They stand in the way of learning to use written language effectively and appropriately for one's own purposes (Brown 1987).

Still another factor impinging on bilingual programs and all that goes on within them, writing included, is the political climate for bilingual education. Relative to the later 1970s, the climate has deteriorated. Federal guidelines for ensuring children's access to education through a language they can understand are ignored; high-ranking federal officials publicly state their opposition to bilingual education; support grows for proposals making English the official language and for curbing any activity (including bilingual education) that would "endanger" the position of English; bilingual education is required to prove its effectiveness (via test scores) to an extent beyond that demanded of other educational "treatments" (Crawford 1987).

These are just a few of the factors that complicate decisions about written language instruction in bilingual programs. Some of these factors maintain the same general look with minor local variations across all bilingual programs (e.g., pressure from testing). Others vary widely from program to program (e.g., particular home languages, extent and type of teachers' experiences with each of the school languages). This variation is behind our premise that highly specified blanket policies are bound to conflict with the particulars in local cases.

If we are urging policy makers to refrain from being bulls in the subtle china shops of individual community language situations, we are not asking them to be idle. Nor are we promoting extreme "home rule." It is imperative to establish broad state and national policies regarding language rights and educational access for discriminated-against (not just numerical) minorities. Policy makers *must* make *general* policies. They must see bilingual education in the light of equity issues as they study the diversity within the many publics. The "temper of the times" and "current political climates" are never monoliths connected automatically to one line of action. They have minor keys and single clarion notes; they shift and change. While policy makers cannot ignore prevailing mentalities, they need not slavishly follow them. They can listen to many voices and then *lead* in establishing general policy. They can also write goals based on deep, consensual wishes. For example, in the United States there is an overwhelming consensus that people want their children to be able to read and write. There is much less agreement on the importance of being able to read particular texts or write particular genres; even less on being able to write particular genres in particular languages. It is up to policy makers to opt for the real (if vague) goal (e.g., "we aim to develop literate people") rather than to mandate multiple trivialized operationalizations that inherently will fail to capture the essence of the original goal. (Specific smaller goals rarely add up to a widely-wished-for ideal. Unfortunately, small supposed subgoals take time away from—and prevent the achievement of—the real one that was wanted all along.) It is equally imperative that policy makers at high governmental levels permit autonomy for those on the local scene, that is, permit local people to develop local policies congruent with broad policies for reaching widely shared goals.

Issues to Be Considered When Developing Local Policies

Being closer to classroom scenes, those making the local decisions about writing curricula in bilingual programs are better able to see details in local language situations, but they also must know what to look at. In the following discussion we are not urging local decision makers to acquiesce to each aspect of the local situation, incorporating, for example, racist language attitudes into curriculum policies simply because such attitudes exist in the community. But we do advise decision makers to acknowledge such a condition in order to plan deliberately to offset it.

What then must be considered in local policies regarding writing in a bilingual program? We see four general questions that must be asked, all of them implicating to some extent people's attitudes toward language in general and written language in particular.

1. What is the nature of written language acquisition?
2. What language resources are available?
3. How are written products treated in each language?
4. What is the value and what are the consequences of being able to write in each language?

Nature of Written Language Acquisition

This first area concerns general principles rather than local conditions. In formulating policies about written language education, the basic question is what is the best current understanding of how language is acquired. From there, policy makers must then come to grips with the details of the local language situations as these relate to the best available notions about written language acquisition.

Like oral language, written language is acquired through actual use. Some of that use occurs during interaction with others who demonstrate while they are actually using written language for real purposes what written language is for and how it works (Smith 1981; Harste, Woodward and Burke 1984). In these interactions, meaning-making is central—with the meanings being made for some purpose of the reader/writer (e.g., for killing time, for getting information, for reminding someone, for warning, for getting attention, for keeping track, etc.). On other occasions, the learner is alone but still using a *social* tool. That is, the written language being used and learned is shaped by a culture, governed by conventions shared by other members of the society, subject to social and historical constraints on how and for what it can be used. As with oral language, what is being learned in written language are the systems of rules/conventions/constraints for exercising freedom-within-cultural-bounds, for making one's own meanings for culturally possible purposes in particular situations. That is, both conventionality and autonomy are critical aspects of oral and written language acquisition. The best "teaching" in oral (Edelsky 1978; Wells 1981) and written (Calkins 1986; Graves 1983; Hudelson 1986; Smith 1981) language acquisition seems to require responding to what the reader/writer is trying to do. This does not mean responding to the child's completion of a worksheet, but to a child's sincere effort to use written language to warn, wonder, inquire, scold, forgive, direct, etc. In order for a learner to have such purposes in school and in order for a teacher to be free to respond to these, both learner and teacher need autonomy to devise their own curricula, to become genuinely engaged. Local decision makers must work hard to encourage the existence of situations in which language can be acquired through real use and eliminate policies that prevent such situations from occurring.

Language Resources

Before making policy decisions about written language in bilingual programs, decision makers must examine the specific context of the local community, including the language resources available to the learners and to the school. Many bilingual educators would argue that the children's primary available language resource is their already developed home language and that this language should be used for initial literacy development. From the perspective of writing and reading as activities in which learners actively compose texts and construct meaning (Lindfors 1987; Tierney and Pearson 1983), learners will come to the composing process with greater built-in language resources to create texts if they are creating them in a language that they control rather than in a language that they are just learning. But learning to write also involves other language resources beyond the oral language itself. One of these resources is texts created by authors other than the learners. These texts will be more or less available depending upon the community language situation.

One reality, common among Native American communities, may be that the native language has never been written down. This situation will mean that bilingual programs will not have available authentic native language texts that learners need, both to read from and to use to construct their own pieces.

A variation of this situation occurs in communities where languages have only recently developed or are still developing and standardizing their written systems. In these cases, relatively few printed materials will have been created. Frequently the creation of texts is delayed by debates about which of several proposed orthographies should be used. For example, some Haitian Creole material in this country is not widely accepted because there is disagreement about which Haitian Creole orthography to accept as the definitive one.

Further, even though native language written texts exist, the community may question the use of the home language in the school. In some cases the use of the language in the school domain is viewed as inappropriate because of the low social status accorded the language. For example, in Haiti, French has a history of high status and prestige; Creole is the lowly language of the poor and uneducated. To this day many Haitians, having internalized the negative attitudes toward Creole, refuse to acknowledge that they speak Creole. These same individuals fight against the use of Creole in the schools and against children learning to write and read in Creole.

In other cases, the question of utilizing language resources concerns not the status but the broader issue of the acceptability of vernacular literacy per se. In the Navajo Nation, for example, Navajo traditionally has been the oral language of the home, community, and tribal activities, with English the written language for almost all situations. Although Navajo literacy was introduced in the early 1900s, it has been slow to take hold. Many Navajos have associated vernacular literacy with governmental, religious, and educational efforts to assimilate the Navajos into mainstream American culture. Therefore, teaching children to write and read in Navajo has been viewed by many as the first step toward cultural assimilation, a situation that has led to conflict over whether to make use of readily available written Navajo texts in bilingual classrooms (Spolsky and Irvine 1982). So while the written language resources may be available, a question remains as to whether they should be used in schools.

Even where the languages in bilingual programs are languages with written traditions, it is often difficult to get the quantity and variety of reading materials that are available in English (Goodman, Goodman and Flores 1979). Few other countries in the world have a children's literature/tradebook industry that rivals that of the United States. There are problems in importing books from other countries, and the books tend to be expensive in comparison to books purchased from the United States. Teachers in Spanish-English bilingual programs often express concern about the relative lack of high-quality children's books original-ly written in Spanish, even though some literature has been identified (Schon 1978). The lack of authentic texts is even more pronounced in less common languages such as Vietnamese and Lao. The question of quantity of materials is also affected by the issue of which dialect certain materials have been written in. This creates real problems in bilingual education programs, as Chicano Spanish speakers complain that they want material written in Chicano or at least Mexican Spanish rather than Cuban or Puerto Rican or Castilian Spanish.

Another complicating factor is the quality of material available in home languages. Learners need real and functional texts (authentic re-sources) that will demonstrate varieties of "book talk" (e.g., style of writ-ten narrative, written exposition, written directions, etc.) and also help them learn to write like readers (e.g., make use of "book talk" as they write, as well as anticipate other readers' responses to their writing) (Goodman 1987). Many of the non-English language texts do not meet the criteria of variety, natural language, and authenticity. Rather, they re-semble American basal reading texts in their approach to literacy (see Goodman et al. 1988 for an extensive critique of basal readers). In some cases, local bilingual programs have even created the "readers" them-selves, translating or adapting the more mechanistic approaches used in English. In Dade County, Florida, for example, *The Miami Linguistic Readers*, a series of phonics materials written originally for English as a second language learners, was adapted into Spanish as part of the Span-ish Curriculum Development Component. Later the same principles of teaching reading through sound-letter correspondences and syllable pat-terns were used in the creation of beginning reading materials in Haitian Creole.

A human language resource of critical importance for teach-ing/learning writing is the teacher. We know that in many "regular" classrooms English speaking teachers do not view themselves as writers and do almost no writing, either for themselves or with their students. One of the assumptions of such in-service education efforts as the Na-tional Writing Project is that, in order to become effective writing teach-ers, teachers must themselves become writers. In other words, to develop literacy in others, teachers must be highly literate themselves. In many bilingual programs, as we have mentioned earlier, teachers have been educated in their second language, and most of the reading and writing that they do occurs in that language. There is a strong possibility, therefore, that teachers do not view themselves as writers in the home language. In fact, many bilingual teachers rather consistently denigrate the variety of home language they speak and lament their lack of ability in that language. If teachers do not view themselves as writers in the home language (indeed, if they do not view themselves even as good speakers), this may affect their support of their students' writing in the home language. And if teachers do not view themselves as writers at all—either in the home language or in English—how will they nurture children in their development as writers?

Children learning to write need access to others who write. Teachers may serve this role if they write themselves. Additionally, one might assume that another source of access to writers would be the local community. But the case of Navajo, described earlier, demonstrates that any such assumption needs to be examined carefully. Where one might assume that Navajo-speaking adults would write in Navajo, in fact that is often not the case. English is the language most often used for writing by Navajos. If children do not see adults using written Navajo for specific individual or social purposes, they are likely to regard writing in Navajo as an exercise—not as written language for life. If children see adults using writing in any language for a very limited number of purposes, they are unlikely to see a wide range of needs for writing or to incorporate "writer" into their identities. As we look at various communities as possible sources for demonstrations of written language, we must ask questions such as these: Who in the community knows how to write? In what languages do people write? What kinds of writing do people do? For what purposes do people write? How can schools both use and *extend* community resources so that children will become writers?

Treatment of Written Products

Research and theory show that writers learn to write by seeing demonstrations of authentic written language by other users, by writing for real and varied purposes, by sharing what they have written with varied audiences, by utilizing the reactions of others to reconsider and revise some of what they create, by working through changes in order to express their intentions in written form. As writers construct meaning, they experiment with forms, generating and testing hypotheses about how written language works and using what they know at that time about written language. Any product a writer produces, therefore, is really a reflection of the ongoing process of creating text. Further, the written products provide evidence of children making use of what they know about written language to work out their ideas, of children solving their problems of expression by using resources available to them, of children controlling the processes of composing.

But not all teachers know this. Many teachers believe that children learn to write by practicing a set of discrete and isolated skills until these have been "mastered." Only then do teachers consider learners able to create text in the sense of working out ideas using written language. Our experience has been that many bilingual program teachers share the latter view of written language acquisition, regardless of whether children are writing in their home or second language (Edelsky 1986; Hudelson 1985). This view may reflect conventional wisdom or professional education (for example, many Spanish-speaking teachers educated in Cuba or Mexico have been taught to teach writing by teaching letter sounds and syllables; many Haitian teachers have learned to direct children to memorize words and take dictation; the writing approach in many United States bilingual programs emphasizes exercises with small segments of language). In any case, evidence mounts that teachers' beliefs about how writing and reading are learned have a direct effect on how they teach (Deford 1985; DeFord and Harste 1982), including how they react to student products and student errors.

As one example, here is a short piece written by a first grade Spanish-speaking child enrolled in a bilingual program that emphasized children's written expression:

Cuando llo se lla grande boyaser
una maestra y boya garar mucho
dinero para comprarles a mistues
ninos les boya conprar ropa y
jugetes

Standard Adult Spanish:

Cuando yo sea grande voy a ser una
maestra. Y voy a ganar mucho dinero
para comprarles a mis ninos. Les
voy a comprar ropa y juguetes.

English translation:

When I am an adult I am going to be
a teacher. And I am going to earn
a lot of money to buy (things) for
my children. I am going to buy them
clothes and toys.

From one perspective this piece could be viewed as a demonstration of creative problem solving, risktaking and using what one knows about the written system of Spanish to express an idea. The child's invented spellings, unconventional segmentation, crossouts, and lack of punctuation might be analyzed in terms of working hypotheses about how written Spanish is organized (Edelsky 1986; Hudelson 1981–82). The piece may be used to analyze what the child knows and thinks about written Spanish. But from a different perspective, the piece could be viewed as riddled with mistakes, as a demonstration of the writer's lack of knowledge of sound-letter correspondences, inability to spell words correctly, laziness about punctuation, and forgetfulness about leaving spaces between words. The piece may be used to judge what the child does not know about standard adult forms of the language, instead of what the child knows. Teachers who believe that products such as the one above show children's inability to write may discourage further experimentation, may fail to promote early and sustained writing experiences, and may, in spite of good intentions, actually prevent a child from learning to write effectively.

Teachers' and parents' views of how people acquire written language will affect how they treat children's written products. These views may also have an effect on the kinds of writing that go on in bilingual classrooms and on the display of this writing. If educators and/or community members believe that writing stories is "a waste of time," this kind of writing may not happen in classrooms. If educators and/or community members are concerned that the use of such writing tools as journals may violate students' rights to privacy (see the SLATE Starter Sheet, October 1985, for a discussion of possible ramifications of the Hatch Amendment), journals may find no place in classrooms. If educators and/or community members believe that to display less than letter-perfect writing (in terms of standard forms) is to "encourage sloppy work" or "provide a bad language model for the others," little work may be displayed around classrooms and schools, and/or the same children's work will always (not) be displayed. These may or may not be realities in any given local setting. Questions need to be asked in order to find out what the local beliefs and actions are; efforts must be made to educate teachers and community members about beliefs that interfere with children's development as written-language users.

Value and Consequences of Writing Ability

Both transitional bilingual programs (bilingual education is offered only until the child can make the transition into an entirely English curriculum) and maintenance bilingual programs (bilingual education is maintained throughout school, with shifting allocation of curriculum between the two languages) claim that first language writing is important. No matter how it is seen—as any entry to the world of literacy, as a bridge to writing in a new language, as a lifelong ability to be nurtured throughout school, as the ability to perform spelling and punctuation exercises, or as the working out of ideas—first language writing has a place in United States bilingual programs. However, having a place does not mean having a place that really counts. Does the first language appear in writing on signs? tests? forms? bulletin boards? Or is it relegated to use on notes to parents who would not otherwise understand? All the various ways print is used in the school affect what is learned about print, including which language has what importance.

The same questions must be asked regarding first language writing outside of school. Being able to write/read in English clearly matters. But what about being able to write in Spanish or Hopi or Chinese? How does first language writing function in the students' community? It is necessary to find out who writes in the first language (their social status, age, gender, societal roles) and for what purposes (whether these are private or public) in order to understand, even in part, how students and their families and their communities will view the inclusion of first language writing in the curriculum.

In general, educators believe that being able to write is empowering. It is necessary (though not sufficient) for access to certain societal resources (e.g., jobs requiring writing) and services initiated or legalized through writing. Educators view writing as a tool for thinking, noting that it offers additional, perhaps unique, opportunities for reasoning, reflection, interactions with oneself. They know that it expands ways of interacting with others, including increasing the possibility of having a public voice. Also, they appreciate that in a society where tested "literacy levels" help promote a myth of meritocracy, test results are the means of distributing rewards; low test scores lead to shame, disempowerment, and an unequal future in the job market.

We concur with these educators. But learning to write in a first language (actually in any language) has these consequences only under certain social conditions (Graff 1987). Moreover, learning to read and write can play havoc with social relations outside the school. For example, in opening up new roles for the writer (and possibilities for new relationships), writing ability in either language can entail social change (Hymes 1972). Understanding and predicting community reaction to students as writers depends on gathering information under the guidance of an ethnography-of-writing perspective (Swzed 1981; Woods-Elliott and Hymes, n.d.). For example, communities of newly-arrived immigrants may not yet have established any stable pattern to their written language use in the new community. English—oral or written—is only one of the many new features these immigrants have to work into their social and intellectual lives. If the native language of these immigrants has included writing, that, too, has been disrupted through immigration since print resources (newspapers, signs, books, etc.) and written language networks have changed. As their children learn to write English, what impact does that have? Does it change their relation to family members or community elders and to family members in interaction with the larger mainstream society? If they learn to write in the home language, but first language writing in the native country was limited by gender or social class, what happens to social roles as writing ability "spreads"? Or do the children refuse to learn to write in the first language rather than violate native norms?

In contrast with communities of new arrivals, communities made up of either indigenous people or long-standing immigrants are more likely to have stable existent patterns of written language use. The question then is whether learning to write in both the first and second language would produce a challenge to the community's language situation. If it does, it is important to identify who wants the change and who does not. In anticipating whether there will be arguments over first language writing in school in indigenous and established immigrant communities, it is equally important to learn whether first language writing will be a red herring. That is, what other community battles (over traditional versus "modern" ways, over separation and nationhood versus annexation) may underlie disagreements over whether or not to teach people to write in the first language, which languages should be taught and for how long, and who should get the instruction.

Conclusion

The picture for writing in bilingual programs is indeed complicated. What happens in any given classroom will be influenced by a host of locally-varying factors arising from many larger contexts. This means that there can be no uniform, highly specified, written language policies or programs that will be effective everywhere. On the other hand, given a combination of local language situation details, neither is there one automatic local policy response. Instead, by addressing the question areas we have identified, local decision makers can gather the information they need to understand the written language situation in their own communities. Armed with that understanding, they can plan for the situation they want; they can plan for change rather than be surprised by it.

References

Brown, R. 1987. Literacy and accountability. *Journal of State Government* 60: 68–72.

Calkins, L. 1986. *The art of teaching writing*. Exeter, NH: Heinemann.

Crawford, J. 1987. Bilingual education: Language, learning and politics. *Education Week* April 1, 1987, 19–50.

DeFord, D. 1985. Validating the construction of theoretical orientation in Reading Instruction. *Reading Research Quarterly* 15: 351–67.

DeFord, D., and J. Harste. 1982. Child Language Research and Curriculum. *Language Arts* 58: 590–600.

Edelsky, C. 1978. "Teaching" oral language. *Language Arts* 55: 291–96.

_____. 1986. *Writing in a bilingual program: Habia una vez*. Norwood, NJ: Ablex.

Edelsky, C., and S. Harman. 1988. One more critique of testing—with two differences. *English Education* 20(1988): 157–71.

Fishman, J. *Bilingual education: An international sociological perspective*. 1976. Rowley, MA: Newbury House.

General Accounting Office. 1987. *Bilingual education: A new look at the research evidence*. Washington, DC: United States Government Printing Office.

Goodman, K. 1987. *What's whole in whole language?* Portsmouth, NH: Heinemann.

Goodman, K., Y. Goodman, and B. Flores. 1979. *Reading in the bilingual classroom: Literacy and biliteracy*. Rosslyn, VA: National Clearinghouse for Bilingual Education.

Goodman, K., P. Shannon, Y. Freeman, and S. Murphy. 1988. *Report card on basal readers*. Katonah, NY: Richard C. Owen Publishers.

Graff, H. 1987. *The legacies of literacy*. Bloomington, IN: Indiana University Press.

Graves, D. 1983. *Writing: Teachers and children at work*. Exeter, NH: Heinemann.

Grosjean, F. 1982. *Life with two languages: An introduction to bilingualism*. Cambridge, MA: Harvard University Press.

Hakuta, K. 1986. *Mirror of language: The debate on bilingualism*. New York: Basic Books.

Harste, J., V. Woodward, and C. Burke. 1984. *Language stories and literacy lessons*. Exeter NH: Heinemann.

Hudelson, S. 1981–82. An investigation of children's invented spelling in Spanish. *NABE Journal* 9: 53–68.

———. 1985. Janice: Becoming a writer of English. ERIC Document ED 249 760, February.

———. 1986. ESL children's writing: What we've learned, what we're learning. In *Children and ESL: Integrating perspectives,* ed. P. Rigg and D.S. Enright. Washington, DC: Teachers of English to Speakers of Other Languages.

———. 1987. The role of native language literacy in the education of language minority children. *Language Arts* 64: 827–41.

Hymes, D. 1972. Introduction, In *Functions of language in the classroom,* ed. C. Cazden, D. Hymes, and V. John. New York: Teachers College Press.

Lindfors, J. 1987. *Children's language and learning*, 2nd ed. Englewood Cliffs, NJ: Prentice Hall.

Meier, D. 1981. Why reading tests don't test reading. *Dissent* 28: 457–66.

Rosier, P., and W. Holm. 1979. *The Rock Point experience: An experiment in bilingual education*. Washington, DC: Center for Applied Linguistics.

Schon, I. 1978. *Books in Spanish for children and young adults*. Metuchen, NJ: Scarecrow Press.

SLATE Starter Sheet. 1985. Urbana, IL: National Council of Teachers of English, October.

Smith, F. 1981. Demonstrations, engagement, and sensitivity. *Language Arts* 58: 103–12.

————. 1973. Twelve easy ways to make learning to read difficult. In *Psycholinguistics and reading,* ed. F. Smith. New York: Holt, Rinehart and Winston.

Spolsky, B., and P. Irvine. 1982. Sociolinguistic Aspects of the Acceptance of Literacy in the Vernacular. In *Bilingualism and language contact: Spanish, English and Native American languages.* ed. F. Barkin, E. Brandt and J. Ornstein-Galicia. New York: Teachers College Press.

Szwed, J. 1981. The ethnography of literacy. In *Writing: The nature, development and teaching of written communication,* Vol. 1, ed. M. Whiteman. Hillsdale, NJ: Lawrence Erlbaum.

Tierney, R., and P. D. Pearson. Toward a composing model of reading. *Language Arts* 60: 568–80.

Troike, R. 1981. Synthesis of research on bilingual education. *Educational Leadership* 14: 498–504.

UNESCO. 1953. *The use of vernacular languages in education.* Paris: UNESCO, 1953.

Wells, G. 1981. *Learning through interaction: The study of language development,* New York: Cambridge University Press.

Woods-Elliott, C., and D. Hymes. Issues in literacy: Different lenses. Unpublished ms.

III

POSSIBILITIES

7

How We Welcome Newcomers and Celebrate Diversity at the Garfield School

William Waxman
Garfield School

The 1980–81 school year was quite normal—320 children in grades kindergarten through eight. No bilingual children, no children of color. Ninety-three percent of the students received free lunch.

In April, 1981, we were notified that approximately one hundred Cambodian families would be moving to our school district in Revere. We immediately called the Massachusetts State Department of Education and pleaded for assistance. They sent two people, Maureen Wark and Marie Eberly, to help us plan a series of after-school workshops designed to familiarize every adult in the building—teachers, custodians, office staff, administrators—with these refugees who would be entering our school. Wark and Eberly located people in the area to help us address the following questions about the newcomers: Who are they? Why are they coming? What have they been subjected to? How can we mobilize the community to embrace these fellow humans?

In the workshops we met with a woman from Newton who had lived in Southeast Asia and a Cambodian teacher who had lived in refugee camps. They taught us to be sensitive to the conditions in the camp and to the cultural ways of our future students. We learned, for example, that stealing is a way of surviving in the camps and that we should deal with this problem but not get too excited about it. We also learned to refrain from touching Cambodian children on the head, a sign of disrespect, and to watch for abrasions on the children's arms caused by coins being rubbed on their skin, a folk-medicine custom.

To prepare for the children's arrival, we obtained a list of their names and ages from the Office of Refugee Resettlement. Each name was given to a Garfield student who was in the same grade and lived on the same street as his or her Cambodian counterpart. The Garfield students were expected to learn how to pronounce the name, find the Cambodian child whose identification tag matched the name they had been given, and be that child's "buddy." Being a buddy meant coming to and going from school together, introducing the newcomers to friends and family, and taking them to their classes.

The Garfield staff agreed that our priority would be integration first and education second. We had to make the children feel wanted and loved. To facilitate the integration process, Savath Sath, who had been the children's teacher in the refugee camp, was hired after receiving a certification waiver from the Department of Education. During the first year, he stayed in the school office to help parents with resettlement problems, such as landlord abuse, and with police procedures. He offered help in areas other than education. Since that time, Mr. Sath has received a bachelor's degree and is now a certified teacher at Garfield.

We spent the entire summer of 1981 registering students as they moved into the community. When school started in September, 1981, 112 new Cambodian students were enrolled. There were many wet eyes witnessing children as they matched identification tags and hugged each other. In the following two years, every new student was immediately paired with a buddy.

To promote interaction between the newcomers and old-timers, a Parent Advisory Council was formed by November 1981, with the help of Mr. Sath. Since most Garfield parents work during the week, the council met on Sundays. One of the functions of the council was to demystify the role of teachers and schools. We discovered that, for Cambodians, teachers have an elevated role, coming second in the hierarchy of respect, right after grandparents. The Cambodian parents were initially reluctant to become involved in their children's education, as they were accustomed to assuming a subservient role vis-à-vis teachers.

At a P.T.A. Executive Board meeting held in January, 1982, it was voted that P.T.A. members would have to visit Cambodian homes and recruit the parents. Current members were required to escort the Cambodian parents to P.T.A. meetings for one year.

In 1983, our seventh- and eighth-grade students were sent to another school because of increased enrollment of Cambodian and Hispanic children. This was also the year we formed the bilingual program that exists to this day. Each grade has a team of teachers consisting of two regular teachers, two ESL teachers, one Cambodian bilingual teacher, and one Chapter I reading teacher. A bilingual child spends one-third of the day in a multiracial nonacademic class, such as gym, music, art, breakfast, lunch, penmanship, antibigotry, self-esteem, cultural awareness, and peer tutoring. They spend another third of the day in a native-speaking class of math, social studies, science, and native language and culture, and the final third in ESL where they are taught English language arts. Part of our philosophy of bilingual education is that all teachers take part in the education of all students, not just those in their native-speaking classes. We wanted the children to see Cambodian and American teachers as role models. So, in ESL classes where ESL teachers have primary responsibility, Cambodian teachers act as aides. And, in Khymy classes, the roles are reversed, with Cambodian teachers playing the key role and ESL teachers acting as aides.

We introduced our summer program in 1985. There were three goals we wanted to accomplish with this program: (1) to offer ESL instruction for our bilingual children and remedial reading for the monolingual children; (2) to encourage the children to play together and enjoy each others' company in a nonacademic atmosphere; and (3) to address the teen racial problem in the neighborhood.

Let's dwell on the teen racial problem. We received a grant from the Massachusetts Department of Education to train twenty high school students to be teacher aides in the summer program. They were recruited because of their bad reputations regarding race relations, paid a generous salary, and paired according to their racial makeup. Each pair, composed of one Cambodian and one black, Hispanic, or white, was assigned to a racially mixed group of children and given the responsibility of teaching race relations. The teens also met for an hour each day with a trained counselor and discussed problems they were having in their neighborhood. We found that even the toughest teenager softens when charged with the responsibility of instructing little children. This program, now in its fifth year, is very successful.

In 1986 we received a grant from the Revere Lottery Arts Council to introduce an afternoon cultural performing-arts program. Children are taught songs and dances from a variety of world cultures. Performers are invited to introduce their art and to perform with the children. The program culminates in an evening of whole-world entertainment and celebration open to the public. One year, there was a one-act ballet with an all-Cambodian cast as well as a Cambodian dance with an all-white cast.

Because of further increases in enrollment, we had to send our fifth- and sixth-grade students to another school in 1987. This was also the year the Massachusetts Department of Education approved the City of Revere's plan to build a new Garfield School to house 1,100 children. Our grade-two children are now participating in a two-way bilingual program in which English-speaking children are learning to communicate in Khymy as the Cambodian children learn to communicate in English.

Without the diligence of the staff, parents, and children, and the assistance of the Massachusetts State Department of Education, we would not have been able to accomplish our goals of integrating the newcomers into our social and academic community. Racial prejudice does not exist in the Garfield School because the members of our community will not tolerate it.

8

Rosa's Challenge
Connecting Classroom and
Community Contexts

Elsa Auerbach and Loren McGrail
University of Massachusetts/Boston

Why I didn't do the homework
Because the phone is ringing
the door is noking
the kid is yumping
the food is burning
time runs fast.

—*Rosa*

Rosa's voice is the voice of many immigrant and refugee students. For them, learning is meaningful to the extent that it relates to their day-to-day reality and helps them act on it. Thus Rosa has pinpointed a profound truth: because the acquisition of literacy always takes place in a social context, teaching must take this context into account. Otherwise it can become one more burden in an already busy life. Rosa is offering us a challenge: as educators, we must constantly connect what happens inside the classroom with what happens outside the classroom and work with students to make literacy a tool for impacting their lives.

Rosa is a student at Boston's Cardinal Cushing Center for the Spanish-Speaking, one of 150 participants in the University of Massachusetts/Boston English Family Literacy Project (FLP). The staff of this project began its work in early 1987 with a firm commitment to taking up Rosa's challenge. We hoped to do this by discovering students' issues and concerns, and making those issues central to their learning so that literacy could become a tool for taking action in their lives. We wanted to do this by developing a participatory process that would involve students in determining the content, processes, and outcomes of the curriculum. In this way, we hoped that the classroom would both model changes in social relations and prepare students for making changes outside the classroom. What follows is an account of how this early commitment to participatory ESL played itself out in practice—what happened as we tried to make our ideal a reality.

Context for the Project

The first important realization we came to in attempting to implement a participatory process is that *the conditions shape the possibilities*. This means that choices made before we ever walk into the classroom will determine to some extent the direction that each class takes. The way that the project is structured, goals are formulated, and recruitment is carried out all influence the development of the curriculum. If a class is made up of students from a single language group, possibilities for bilingual exploration of issues exist; if a class consists only of parents, content may focus on child-rearing or schooling. If a class takes place in a housing project, the dynamics and expectations will differ from those in a formal school setting or adult education site. The world of the classroom does not exist in a vacuum, and we need to be responsive to these conditions.

In our own case, the project structure was somewhat complex and created a particular set of contradictions that we had to address in developing our approach. Ours was one of many projects funded by the Office of Bilingual Education and Minority Language Affairs through Title VII, the Bilingual Education Act, to provide English literacy instruction to the parents of children in bilingual education programs. While some of these projects are school-based, ours is not. The classes take place in three community-based adult literacy centers with no formal connection to the public school system. The project's aim is to enhance the ESL literacy proficiency of parents so that they can participate more actively in their children's education.

Our project is a community-university collaboration. While the university applied for and administers the funding, classes are fully integrated into the adult literacy programs where they are housed, with hiring, recruitment, and scheduling done according to the procedures of each site. Teachers are based at the community centers but meet weekly with those from the other sites to discuss common issues.

Since each site has its own procedures for recruitment and placement, classes vary in size, level, and ethnic composition. We decided early on that rather than creating rigid entry criteria to simplify our work, ensure uniform classes, and facilitate implementation (turning students away who didn't narrowly fit predetermined specifications), we would take students as they came, attempting to meet *their* needs. This meant accepting students into our classes who were members of extended families rather than only the biological parents. Many refugee and immigrant families have been torn apart by the traumas of war and migration; the notion of a nuclear family doesn't correspond to the living situations of our students. As a result, students in our classes include parents, grandparents, aunts and uncles, and sometimes unrelated caregivers living in households with bilingual children ranging in age from preschool to high school. We have taught up to twenty-six language groups at a time; only one site serves a single language group. Class sizes range from twelve to thirty; levels range from no prior schooling or literacy in the first language and beginning ESL to educated intermediate students.

Thus our classes are like those of many community-based adult ESL programs in makeup and diversity, with the added dimension of a mandate to focus on family literacy content. These particular conditions gave rise to a dilemma for us. On the one hand, our funders wanted us to develop a "family literacy" curriculum; on the other, we felt committed to centering curriculum content around the needs and issues that students identified. The diversity of the student population didn't lend itself to a unified core of issues and, in particular, to a narrow interest in parent-child literacy activities. Thus we were faced with the question: How could we be true to a student-centered participatory approach *and* to our obligation to focus on family literacy content?

Similar contradictions may arise for anyone attempting to implement a participatory curriculum. For a work-place program, there may be tension between employers' expectations and workers' goals. For a first-language literacy class, there might be a contradiction between the teacher's commitment to developing the first language as a basis for English literacy and the students' desire to get into English literacy as soon as possible.

The key to addressing this type of dilemma is realizing that just as we hope students will examine the social context of their lives, we, as educators, need to examine the social context of our work. *The starting point for a participatory curriculum project must be some analysis of the context of the project itself.* This means that educators must ask questions like these: What are the goals of this project, class, or curriculum from the funders', administrators', students', and teachers', points of view? How and why did this project come into being? What is the political agenda of the various participants? For example, why does the employer want a program for immigrant workers? Why does the government want prevocational training for refugees? What are the implicit expectations for students and their futures? In our own project, we asked questions like these: Why are policy makers focusing on family literacy now? What are the assumptions of current program models? How do these assumptions relate to the realities of family contexts for literacy acquisition?

As we began to analyze the social context for our project, we found that the prevailing rationale for projects like ours is that the current literacy crisis can be largely attributed to family inadequacies. The assumptions are that parents aren't literate, don't value literacy, and don't have the skills they need to help their children, thereby creating an "intergenerational cycle of illiteracy" in which the "disease" of illiteracy is passed from one generation to the next. Homes of poor, minority, and immigrant children are often characterized as "literacy-impoverished," with few reading materials, little value placed on reading, and minimal parental support for literacy development.

According to this rationale, programs need to teach parents "how to do structured academic activities that reinforce schoolwork" (Simich-Dudgeon 1987, 3). As a result, the dominant family literacy model focuses on activities like helping with homework, reading report cards, interacting with teachers, and understanding the American school system.

A further assumption is that what the schools are doing is fine and that parents need to do more of the same at home. But when we looked at studies of what actually happens in the homes of successful readers, we found that this assumption isn't borne out (Auerbach 1989). What differentiates homes of successful vs. unsuccessful readers is not that parents do this kind of add-on literacy work, but rather that they integrate literacy in a variety of ways into the fabric of everyday life so that it becomes socially significant as a tool for dealing with day-to-day concerns (Taylor 1983). In addition, the Harvard Families and Literacy study (Snow 1987) showed that after grade three, even the most supportive home environments couldn't make up for poor schooling, and in these cases, a critical factor in literacy development was advocacy: the degree to which parents voiced their concerns to teachers and other school authorities.

Taken together, these studies suggest a very different approach, one in which family literacy programs start with family and community-determined needs. Instead of a "from the school to the community and family" model (which attempts to transform culturally-diverse home contexts into sites for mainstream literacy practices), they suggest a "from the family and community to the school" model that (1) explores and builds on existing community and family strengths, concerns, and practices; (2) acknowledges socioeconomic problems that families face as legitimate concerns; (3) broadens the ways literacy is socially significant in family life by using it as a tool to address these concerns; (4) supports childrens' literacy development by modeling positive practices with parents; (5) fosters the development of critical analysis and advocacy in dealing with issues of schooling; and (6) develops participatory classroom relationships as the basis for participation in community life.

Thus this kind of social analysis of the context for family literacy helped us to address our dilemma and realize that there is no contradiction in trying to be both a family literacy project and a participatory one. It led us to the understanding that, in fact, a participatory approach to family literacy may be more powerful than the dominant model because it diversifies literacy uses and interactions instead of narrowly limiting them to parent-child literacy activities. The remainder of this chapter will present some of the principles and processes for putting this understanding into practice.

The Curriculum Development Process

Since a participatory approach is based on incorporating community cultural forms and social issues into the content of literacy activities, curriculum development is, by definition, context-specific, built on the particular conditions, concerns, and contributions of specific groups of students. As such, it doesn't involve a predetermined curriculum, itemization of skills, set of structures, materials, texts, or outcomes. Where a more traditional curriculum starts by identifying particular outcomes (ends) and prescribing a plan (means) for achieving these outcomes, this emergent, negotiated curriculum develops through ongoing, collaborative investigation of critical issues in students' lives (Sauvé 1986). As these issues emerge, they are explored and transformed into content-based instruction using a variety of tools and resources. In this process, the "curriculum" is more of a hypothesis than a road map. Its function is to give teachers a sense of structure and direction, but equally important is the expectation that they won't stick to it (Candlin 1984). Outcomes are often unexpected and action-oriented. The direction and form that actions take emerge from discussion, reflection, and negotiation and, as such, cannot be predicted.

The tentative, emergent nature of a participatory curriculum doesn't mean, however, that a teacher goes into the classroom empty-handed. In order to implement this type of curriculum development process, there are several things teachers need: first is a conceptualization of why they are embarking on this endeavor and an overview of the process; second is a set of tools and procedures for finding and developing student themes into literacy work; third is a set of resources, including both materials and coworkers. One of the most important aspects of our work has been the sharing between teachers. Talking about what is going on in the classroom is perhaps the single most critical resource for developing a participatory approach.

The "why" of a participatory approach comes from adult learning and literacy theory. As Knowles (1984) and others have pointed out, adult education is most effective when it is experience-centered, related to real needs, and directed by learners themselves. Freire (1973) argues that adult literacy can be either domesticating or empowering. When the skills, processes, and outcomes are determined *for* students, they become passive objects of their own education. Freire calls this a *problem-solving* approach, in which the educator/expert, by prescribing and transmitting answers or solutions (in the form of skills, behaviors, or competencies), effectively silences student voices.

When, on the other hand, students are engaged at every step in determining the content, processes, and outcomes, they become subjects of their learning. When the knowledge is jointly constructed by participants, literacy becomes a tool in not only finding voice but in using it to act in the world. Freire calls this a *problem-posing* approach: the teacher poses problems based on students' reality and guides them through a process of dialogue and critical reflection on that reality from which they generate their own group alternatives for dealing with the problems.

Armed with this understanding, the teacher works to facilitate a process of engaging students in their own education, creating contexts for this construction of knowledge and using literacy as a meaningful tool in addressing student concerns. While the particular ways this happens differ in every classroom and for every group of students, there are four main components to the process: (1) finding critical themes and concerns in students' lives; (2) extending language and literacy development through the exploration of these themes; (3) taking action to address the issues; and (4) evaluating the process.

An early misconception we had in our project was that these steps occur in a linear, sequential order, starting with an extended period of identifying and "collecting" issues, then developing a core set of units around these issues, and moving sequentially through the units with each including phases of dialogue, participatory classroom activities, actions outside the classroom, and group evaluation. This view came in part from the process described by Freire where the literacy worker becomes immersed in the students' community for a period of months in order to know that community and then proceeds to identify themes and transform these themes into "codifications" (abstract representations of the themes) as the basis for dialogue, decoding, and action.

The reality of the adult ESL classroom doesn't usually allow for this model because students come from different backgrounds, language groups, parts of the city, and occupations. The classroom itself may be the only community that students have in common. Hence, the identification of issues often emerges as a *result* of classroom interaction rather than as a *precondition* to it. Further, because teachers are often part-time, underpaid, and not involved in intake or assessment, the possibilities for outside investigation are minimal. In addition, we have found that issues never exist in a vacuum; they are situated in time and have power only because of the particular context from which they emerge. What starts as a loaded, energizing issue one week may, for unpredictable reasons, lose its wind and die the next week, never moving toward action. Finally, our experience has been that evaluation can easily become the neglected stepchild of the process unless it is built in on a regular basis such as weekly or monthly. Thus, more realistic than a sequence of extended phases is the notion of a series of short-term cycles, each of which starts with the emergence of a theme that is immediately explored through participatory literacy activities and sometimes followed by action and evaluation. A description of some of the activities we use and the issues we face in moving through these cycles follows.

Finding Themes and Issues

There are a number of ways that student concerns can be identified. What won't work, however, is asking students directly what they want to do. Often students have no idea what they want to study beyond generic skills (reading, writing, grammar, etc.). Or, they have internalized the very model of "good education" that has excluded them in the past—the teacher-fronted transmission-of-knowledge-and-skills model. Thus teacher-initiated activities designed to uncover issues are often needed, activities that we call *catalysts* or *ways in*. They may be structured activities that, on the surface, look like traditional language lessons (substitution drills, etc.) but allow for student input. In one class, for example, the sentence completion exercise "I like my job because _____ /I don't like my job because _____ " elicited an outburst of response with students generating a long list of concerns leading to further exploration of issues of working conditions, pay, and lack of respect for immigrant workers.

Beyond this type of structured activity, more open-ended catalysts include asking students to talk or write about thematically-loaded photos, create time lines of their life journeys, draw pictures of work or housing or health-care situations, and write dialogue journals in which they talk about issues of importance in their lives.

However, despite our best efforts to elicit themes, the most powerful ones usually emerge when least expected—before, during, or after class in informal conversation, in the time that "doesn't count" as real classwork. The most useful tool for finding "ways in" to literacy work may be what we call *conscious listening*— an openness to letting spontaneous discussion take its own course, to hearing what's hidden between the lines in side comments, to letting students burst into their native language and explore an idea without feeling pressure to get back to "what we're supposed to be doing."

But herein lies a dilemma: very often, students feel that this kind of "diversion" doesn't count—that it's interesting but not *real* language work. Since we claim that our approach is student-directed, how do we respond to this? The key to legitimizing this kind of spontaneous talk is follow-up—consciously keeping track of these diversions and developing literacy activities from them. Again, however, there are no easy prescriptions. The teacher may decide not to follow up on an issue immediately because it is an interruption of something important, because he or she doesn't feel comfortable with it or doesn't know how to pursue it, or because students' energy doesn't sustain itself. The issue may then present itself weeks later, in another context where the follow-up does make sense. Or the class may never get back to it. Part of the art and the challenge of a participatory approach is knowing when to follow up on themes, when to drop them, and when to come back to them. Since there are no rules for this and it's an art which develops over time, teacher-sharing is essential, providing a context for figuring out whether and how to develop particular issues as they arise.

In our own classes, four main categories of themes or issues have emerged through this process: (1) those related to the classroom and educational process itself; (2) those related to family and community interactions around language, literacy, and schooling (language use in the family, attitudes toward the home language and bilingual education, parents as teachers, interactions around homework); (3) those related to the home culture (customs, beliefs, issues of cultural maintenance vs. assimilation); and (4) those related to the broader social context (work, housing, health, the immigration law, discrimination by authorities). During one week, for example, the following issues came up in our classes: protesting a local school closing; developing a housing-project newsletter; beliefs about the solar system; the story of the Virgin of Guadalupe; working conditions for house/office cleaners; a Hispanic parents' advocacy group; and herbal vs. "modern" medicine.

Extending Themes through Participatory Activities

One of the goals of participatory education is to increasingly involve students in deciding how to develop themes. Again, however, we are immediately confronted with a contradiction: when we ask students to make decisions about activities or materials, or to produce their own materials, very often the response is, "You're the teacher; you should know—whatever you think is best." Because their experience has been in teacher-fronted and teacher-directed classrooms, that's what they are most comfortable with and think is "right." Becoming activists in their own learning involves reconceptualizing what education is.

We've tried to address this issue in a variety of ways. First, whenever possible we make this dilemma itself explicit as *content* for dialogue and literacy work. One way is by presenting photos of different learning situations—traditional teacher-fronted classes, people learning in groups where there is no obvious leader, parents teaching children, or children learning from each other. The pictures frame discussion and writing about how people feel in different settings for learning or how students themselves are teachers. In addition, issues of classroom dynamics like use of the first language, the role of corrections, and attendance are themselves codified into dialogue or sociodrama format. Students consciously address these issues as they develop language and literacy.

But it takes time for students to feel comfortable about assuming more responsibility for shaping the curriculum. Becoming involved in producing the actual tools (materials and activities) for extending language and literacy is gradual and must start with the familiar. Our own classes integrate very traditional-looking, teacher-directed activities with more participatory ones. What follows is a toolkit of activities that teachers can draw from in developing each theme. They are presented here along a continuum from most teacher-controlled to most student-controlled as a way of conceptualizing movement toward an increasingly participatory curriculum. For any given issue, the class may use one of these tools or many, depending on their level of engagement.

1. Teacher-selected Published Materials   Teachers can take excerpts from textbooks or "authentic" texts (literature, autobiographies, newspapers, etc.) that relate to a theme and create reading and/or writing activities that link the materials to students' own experiences. Examples we've used include short passages from *Woman Warrior* (Hong Kingston 1978) about work, schooling, and culture conflict, and excerpts from *Don't Be Afraid Gringo* (Alvarado 1987), a testimonial account of the life of a Honduran peasant woman dealing with such issues as labor organizing, marriage, and social roles. Teachers often use newspaper articles about students' home countries, neighborhoods, or schools, modifying or simplifying them for lower-level students and dividing articles into sections for different groups to work on.

2. Teacher-written Texts/Codes   Teachers can create class-specific materials based on issues they have identified through listening to students. These teacher-written texts may vary from short stories, to "Dear Abby" letters, to dialogues or sociodramas, but, whatever the form, the rationale stems from Freire's notion of *re*-presenting a loaded issue in simplified, depersonalized form as the basis for reflection, dialogue, and action. Wallerstein (1983) describes how to develop and use these issue-centered "codes" in depth.

3. Collaborative Student-Teacher Materials   As students explore their own ideas about themes, teachers and students can work together to create texts. Teachers can elicit student ideas on themes (through brainstorming and semantic clustering activities, responses to teacher-selected readings or codes) and then use student-generated words, sentences, and ideas in writing passages that summarize these discussions in collaborative stories. Following the Language Experience Approach (Rigg 1987), students can dictate stories or passages to teachers, which then are reproduced as texts for further dialogue and language/literacy work.

4. Student-written Materials   Students can create their own materials that, in turn, become texts for other students. Student writing may range from informal picture-labeling, journal writing and free writing to interclass letter-writing, and more polished products that go through numerous revisions, editing, and publishing, following a writing process approach. They may include autobiographical accounts of personal experience, fables and stories from the homeland, issue-centered, argumentative writing, or more public texts like individual and group letters to authorities and drafts of speeches for public testimony. Texts may be published together in thematic collections or printed in class newsletters. Students from different classes can exchange texts, contribute to center newsletters, and develop ongoing exchanges.

5. Oral Histories Students can create oral-history texts by interviewing each other, members of their families, members of their communities, and members of other immigrant groups. The interviews can be taped, transcribed, edited, and written about. The collected oral histories then can become the basis for social analysis of similarities and differences between life experiences.

6. Photo-stories Photography can be used in a variety of ways including labeling pictures, writing family stories, taking pictures, and producing photo-stories as the basis for writing. Strohmeyer and McGrail (1988) have described in detail how students from the FLP developed their own writing through a photography project. Barndt and her Canadian colleagues (Barndt et al. 1982) have done extensive work producing photo-stories with their students. They have also involved students in participatory song-writing, video, and sociodrama projects.

Action
We also struggled with the misconception that classroom interaction around each issue must culminate in some form of concrete, visible action outside the classroom—that addressing an issue doesn't "count" in a Freirean sense if it isn't followed by some immediate attempt to change the social context. Again, practice has taught us that if we measure ourselves by this standard, the instances of "action" are few and far between. Many issues never make it beyond the door of the classroom.

Does this mean that change is not taking place, that we've fallen short? Our experience is that change takes many forms, both inside and outside the classroom, and may not be packaged in discrete actions but rather in the gradual, cumulative building of confidence, validation of experience, and change in perspective. Very often it takes months or even years of germination before students are ready to move outside the classroom with their actions. During this time, the changing social relations within the classroom, the critical examination of day-to-day reality, and the development of language and literacy are all serving as a rehearsal for external action. One of our students, for example, after two years in a class that focused heavily on issues of literacy and schooling, became involved in a Hispanic parents' organization working for change in the Boston public schools. She attends meetings with the superintendent, press conferences, and organizational meetings and is working to involve her classmates. Her participation didn't result directly from a "unit" or a "code" but rather from many months of dialogue and from the support and understanding she gained from her class.

Actions our students have taken inside the classroom include telling the teacher they are sick of an issue, improving attendance as a result of dialogue, choosing to write in the first language as an affirmation of identity, and developing guidelines for discussion of personal issues. Students have participated in hiring, program evaluation, fundraising, and planning in their centers. Outside actions have included testifying at public hearings about funding, writing letters to public officials, meeting with school authorities, meeting with students from other centers to discuss issues of common concern, participating in conferences, and reading their own writing at public events.

Evaluation

A goal in participatory education is for students to be involved in evaluating their own learning. This means developing a metalanguage of evaluation, with students talking about what they like, don't like, have learned, and want to learn. Very different from the traditional pre- and post-testing model, this kind of evaluation is integrated as an ongoing part of instructional content. It is a qualitative, two-way process with students and teachers evaluating each other as well as themselves, rather than students being evaluated by teacher-testers. As such, it is not easily reduced to numbers, grade levels, test scores, or funders' expectations.

Because this kind of participatory, qualitative evaluation is virgin territory, traditional views of student roles, lack of experience with metatalk, and language constraints all present challenges to its implementation. Our own preliminary efforts to involve students include wall posters where students write up "I liked _____ , I didn't like _____ " at the end of a class; "Class Accomplishments," a weekly newspaper that summarizes the activities, issues, and problems of the week and in turn becomes a text for further literacy work; writing folders where students collect writings throughout the term and look over them to assess changes at the end of the cycle; and discussions and writings about individual and group progress.

Putting It All Together: Exploring the Context

The following is an account of how this curriculum development process played itself out in one of our classrooms (Loren's), moving, in this case, from catalyst to code to dialogue to writing. It is an account of what it means to listen to students both in terms of content (ideas) and process (how the class should proceed). It also provides evidence that support or advocacy of literacy in families is not only from parent to child but sometimes from child to parent. To capture nuances of why an activity goes the way it does, we're presenting Loren's reflections as a first-person narrative.

> *This cycle began when one day I came upon a very interesting entry in one of my student's journals. The entry was as follows:*

>> My husdpan speak to me in English. And I understand everything he said to me. But I didn't speak to him in English because I don't want he see my mistake. Because I embarese in front of him. He speak to me in English and I speak to him in Spanish. Only I speak in English with my daughter. And the people in the street. When I go to the hospital and when I go to my daughter school because her teacher speak in English.

> *I found the entry provocative and rich in detail. Why did she feel embarrassed to speak in English with her husband? Why was he speaking in English to her in the first place? Why was she more comfortable with her daughter or people on the street? The entry also made me think of different ways we can all be perceived as being like the husband in this entry, the ways we can unknowingly censor or prohibit others from expressing themselves. Sometimes as an English teacher I have felt like this husband speaking in English, knowing the student understands me but won't speak back to me. When I wrote back to Carmen, I asked her if she would share her writing with the class because I thought that other students might be having a similar experience and that we could talk about it so that we could collectively come up with possible strategies for dealing with these feelings of embarrassment and for maximizing the positive moments when they occur. Carmen said she wouldn't mind sharing her writing, but that I had to proofread it first and correct all the spelling and grammar errors.*

> *So a few days later I came back to class with the corrected version and a set of questions to go along with it. Her writing struck me as being a "perfect code" in Freirean terms. All I had to do was think up some appropriate questions that would engage the students in dialogue around this issue. This is what I came up with:*

>> My husband speaks to me in English. And I understand everything he says to me but I don't speak to him in English because I don't want to make mistakes because I am embarrassed in front of him. He speaks to me in English and I speak to him in Spanish. Only, I speak in English to my daughter and the people in the street or when I go to the hospital or my daughter's school because her teacher speaks English.

Questions

1. Is the writer a man or woman?

   What language does she use to speak to her husband?

   What language does she use to speak to her daughter?

   What other people does she speak English with? Why?

   Why does she speak English when she goes to her daughter's school?

2. Why does her husband speak English to her?

   Why does she speak Spanish to him?

   Why is she embarrassed?

   Why does she speak English to her daughter?

3. Have you ever felt embarrassed about speaking English? Describe what happened.

   How do you think her daughter feels? Do you have children?   How do you feel speaking English with them?

   How do you think her husband feels? Have you ever felt like him before?

4. When are you most comfortable speaking English? Why?   When are you least comfortable speaking English? Why?   What can you do to feel more comfortable about speaking   English?

   What is your native language? When do you speak it and   with whom?

Follow-up Activities

Write in the voice of the husband or the daughter about how you think they might feel.

Write a dialogue between the husband and the wife using two languages.

As you can see, the questions follow the classic problem-posing format, moving from the superficial or literal to the personal to the sociopolitical. You peel away layer after layer like an onion until you get to the center—action. In this case, I saw action in terms of the students writing more about this situation as action. Thinking about strategies to make themselves feel less threatened or embarrassed when they spoke in English was also a form of action.

The class went well. As I had hoped, everyone seemed quite familiar with this kind of situation. There was much discussion and testimony about what it was like to be taking an ESL class and how it was changing their roles at home. When I asked which of my suggested follow-up writing activities they wanted to do, however, none of them wanted to do any. Perplexed and hurt a little bit at first, I asked what they did want to do. They said they wanted to write about what we had just been discussing as it related to their own homes. So they wrote, shared, and rewrote their pieces with great interest and attention. Early on, I suggested we collect these writings and put them together and make a book for ourselves. This idea appealed to everyone and acted as a great motivation for students to spend time revising their pieces.

During this writing and rewriting period, I continued responding to weekly journal writings. One day in one of my students' journals, there was an entry that she had clearly not written. When I asked about it, the student confessed it was her daughter's writing and that her daughter often helped her with her homework. I told her that was fine, except that journals were supposed to be private, a dialogue just between the two of us. I suggested that if the daughter wanted to correspond with me, I would be happy to give her another journal to give to her daughter so that she too could write to me. About a week later, much to my surprise, she came in with the journal from her daughter in which her daughter had written to me at great length about her life as a fourteen-year-old. In addition to telling me about her favorite singers and TV shows, she told me about not being able to speak or write more Spanish than she did. She also quite openly told me how she felt about her mother going back to school. The following excerpt expresses it best:

> I'm glad my mother is going to school so she could speak English. It finally mean that I don't have to translate for her ... it must be hard for you to teach the students. You'll also got to be patient ... I really can't do that. I'll never be a good teacher because I'm not good at teaching.

The daughter's directness about her relief in being able to give up her role as translator added another dimension to this issue of what language(s) we should be using, when, and why. I talked to the group about her entry, and it brought up a whole new but related issue— bilingualism in the home. This became the seed for our next cycle of literacy work and also the inspiration for some students to write more candidly about how their kids feel about their learning English.

An example of this kind of openness can be seen in Rosa's work below.

At Home
I talk to my kids about school.
I ask...*Como se portatron?*
They say very good.

> I continue to ask
> about the food...and the homework.
> They speak to me in English...
> I say I am sorry...
> *Yo no endendi nada; por favor hablame*
> *en Espanol* ...The older boy says OK ...OK
> You study english you are supposed to
> understand. They repeat again to me
> slowly and more clearly. *Yo les digo*
> *Muchas gracias...* I love you.

This cycle has no neat ending. Rosa continues to struggle with language issues inside and outside her family. Now she is attending community college. Many of her classmates have had their writings published in a local literary magazine, and, as mentioned previously, one student is working with an Hispanic parents' advocacy group.

We have learned that this "unfinished business" is an essential part of participatory education. Just as we can't go into a teaching situation knowing exactly what will happen, we can't come out of it with neatly packaged positive or negative outcomes. Reducing results to numbers undermines the essence of participatory education — namely, that it is a gradual process of changing social relations. This means letting go of control and recognizing that the measure of having attained our ideal is not necessarily immediately evident test scores or actions, but rather the invisible learning that we may never see. For students like Rosa, it means continuing to challenge us to link learning to its social context and use this learning for purposes she determines herself. For both teachers and students, it means making social analysis an explicit part of the content of our work.

Note: The work reported on in this chapter is the result of collaboration with UMass/English Family Literacy project staff, Ann Cason, Rosario Gomez-Sanford, Loren McGrail, Andrea Nash, and Madeline Rhum. We owe a special debt of gratitude to the students whose work appears in the chapter and to the many others who taught us about their ways of learning and teaching. We would also like to thank Candace Mitchell for her insightful critique of earlier drafts of this chapter.

References

Alvarado, E. 1897. Don't be afraid, Gringo: A Honduran woman
    speaks from the heart. San Francisco: The Institute for Food and
    Development Policy.

Auerbach, E.R. 1989. Toward a social-contextual approach to family literacy.
    Harvard Educational Review, 59 (2): 165–81.

Barndt, D., F. Cristall, and d. marino. (1982). Getting there. Toronto: Between the Lines.

Canklin, C.N. 1984. Syllabus design as critical process. In *General English Syllabus Design,* ed. C.J. Brumfit. Oxford: Pergamon Press.

Freire, P. (1973). Education for critical consciousness. New York: Seabury Press.

Kingston, M.H. 1978. *The woman warrior,* New York: Vintage.

Knowles, M. 1984. *Andragogy in action.* San Francisco: Jossey -Bass.

Rigg, P. 1987. Using the language experience approach with ESL adults. *Literacy in a Second Language: Special Issue of Literacy Exchange.* New South Wales Adult Literacy Council.

Sauvé, V. 1986. Vision in context; The situating of an ESL/EFL curriculum *TESL Canada Journal.* Special Issue 1: 111–25 (Nov.).

Simich-Dudgeon, C. 1987. Involving LEP parents as tutors in their children's education. *ERIC/CLL News Bulletin,* 10:2 (March).

Snow, C. 1987. Factors influencing vocabulary and reading achievement in low-income children. In *Toegepaste Taalwetenschap in Artikelen Special 2.* ed. R. Apple. Amsterdam: ANELA.

Strohmeyer, B., and L. McGrail 1988. *On focus: Photographs and writings by students.* Boston: Cardinal Cushing Center.

Taylor, D. 1983. *Family Literacy: Young children learning to read and write.* Exeter, NH: Heinemann Educational Books.

Wallerstein, N. 1983. Language and culture in conflict: *Problem-posing in the ESL classroom.* Reading, MA: Addison Wesley.

9

A Collaborative Model for Empowering Nontraditional Students

Teri Haas, Trudy Smoke, and José Hernández

Hunter College, City University of New York

The purpose of this chapter is to describe a collaboration between teachers from two developmental writing courses (Haas and Smoke), a peer tutor from the writing lab (Tsouchlarakis) and a social science instructor (Hernandez) teaching a course entitled "Conquered Peoples in America" at an urban college. All students enrolled in the writing courses were also registered for the "Conquered Peoples" course. Since much of the teachers' collaboration evolved through conversation, this chapter will follow the same form. It is transcribed from a series of conversations by the participants discussing and evaluating the project. The peer tutor's responses are included in the appendix to this chapter. Materials used in the course are cited in the references.

Rationale

HERNÁNDEZ: Teaching and learning at our college is typical of public postsecondary institutions that recruit two population groups not well integrated into American intellectual life. The first group consists of those Americans commonly called "minorities," such as African Americans, Puerto Ricans, Native Americans, and Mexican Americans; the second is made up of immigrants from all parts of the world who today make up about one-third of the students taking our classes. These two groups compose a population that is called "nontraditional," insofar as they have a language that is at least partially at variance with standard English and certainly because their cultural backgrounds set them apart from the majority of college students and teachers.

HAAS: These students are usually the first of their families to attend college.

HERNÁNDEZ: Right. And they're highly motivated people who recognize that if they do not succeed in college, their destiny in the United States economy is bleak.

SMOKE: One of the problems is that even though students may enter the college highly motivated, some of them are required because of scores on placement tests to repeat developmental writing and reading many times. When they don't take content courses for several semesters, they become very discouraged; they worry that they will never begin real college work. This was one of the problems that we faced when we originally met to discuss the possibility of joining our courses.

HERNÁNDEZ: Many colleges bar nontraditional students from content courses in all disciplines until they've passed developmental reading and writing courses and assessment tests.

HAAS: The flaw to that thinking is that students may drop out because they feel they're not learning anything new.

HERNÁNDEZ: College is supposed to be an exciting time when your mind is opened to a whole series of new considerations.

HAAS: Yet students do need to gain reading and writing fluency.

SMOKE: Students often need practice in study skills. They haven't learned to take notes. At the beginning of the semester when they're given a list of readings and told to schedule these over the semester, they don't know how to allocate time for these readings, when to study for exams, how to do research papers or to use libraries. They also feel daunted by these skills; this is one reason they drop out very quickly when they are finally permitted to take content courses.

HERNÁNDEZ: The textbooks are often intimidating, too, for inexperienced readers.

HAAS: Our students need to develop advanced literacy, yet they are excluded from intellectually stimulating college courses.

SMOKE: Pairing our courses with José's three-credit introductory social science course offered a solution. In our paired courses, students were reading and writing complex material. They were active learners, listening to lectures, taking notes, and reading and writing about rich material.

HAAS: The content of our paired courses was the students' cultures. They felt included. They could compare your lectures, José, with their lives.

SMOKE: Yes, nontraditional students come to college with a wealth of experience, with a culture of their own, and they're made to feel that these experiences aren't useful. Work in our paired courses drew upon their own culture and experience and, therefore, enabled students to feel that they had a place in the college and important issues to write, think, and read about.

HAAS: My students were enthusiastic about the class.

SMOKE: Mine, too. I had a thirty-two-year-old student from Puerto Rico who worried that he was not going to succeed in college. He started to contribute to the course when we discussed the Puerto Rican poet, Pedro Pietri (1974), whose poems were assigned by José. The student knew Pietri and brought in a tape of Pietri's poetry. This student also belonged to a music group that had performed at the Museum of Natural History, and he brought in a video tape of his group's performance of Puerto Rican music. His experiences became validated in the class. Other students addressed questions to him. He had lived in Puerto Rico and in the United States, and he compared the two experiences. He talked about why he believed his child should be bilingual. He really became alive in class, his writing got better, and he appeared less alienated from the college community.

HAAS: When students become more active, because they have experiences to contribute to class conversation, they also become more assertive. They take charge of their own learning as Freire advocates (1988).

Curriculum

HERNÁNDEZ: My course, "Conquered Peoples in America," describes the consequences of nineteenth-century United States' expansion and compares the Puerto Rican experience to that of Native Americans, Chicanos, and Pacific Island peoples, specifically the Filipinos and Native Hawaiians. It expresses the common situation among these groups who lost control over their homelands, describes their cultures, and provides a detailed study of their colonization. We examine how these groups have maintained their cultural integrity and are currently struggling to attain equality in American society. We also discuss the role of women in these cultures, in which women were equal to men before the European conquest. My basic notion is to empower students, most of whom are women, by helping them recognize their backgrounds and develop self-determination through ethnic and gender identity.

SMOKE: Students changed during the semester. Puerto Rican students became prouder of their heritage. Other ethnic groups illustrated more insight into what it means to be Puerto Rican. They claimed they had thought that the Puerto Rican experience was very different from their own. But by the end of the course these students told me: "We have a lot in common. We've fought similar battles. We have similar prejudices." Some Haitian and Asian students commented on a similarity of family values.

HERNÁNDEZ: The course begins with two strands: the English colonization that led to the Anglo culture and the Spanish conquests that led to the Latin American culture. I give the characteristics and compare these two cultures. That's the first part of the course;

students see the influence of these two cultures on the native inhabitants, beginning with the Native Americans. It's a challenge to get students interested in peoples who are remote from New York City.

HAAS: My students were especially interested in Native Americans after the women from the Mohawk Nation spoke to the class.

HERNÁNDEZ: She tells students what it means to be an American Indian.

HAAS: Last semester my class met after yours, José, and students usually discussed your lectures. They were excited after hearing this woman. She discussed the woman's role in Mohawk culture, didn't she?

SMOKE: She is an elder, which means spiritual and political leader. She explained that traditionally there was gender equality in Native American life. She traces some of today's problems involving male and female roles, such as unemployment and alcoholism, to the sudden shift to the European belief in Christianity, which she perceives as denying gender equality.

HERNÁNDEZ: Christianity and other European beliefs were antithetical to the Mohawks, who have always had a constitutional democracy in which men, women and children participate. By tradition, they believe that a good person lives at one with the universe, in peace and harmony with other peoples.

HAAS: When my students became interested in Native Americans, I assigned *Black Elk Speaks* (1979), in which an Oglala Sioux medicine man describes his tribe's culture and its conflicts with the Europeans. One of the most successful reading and writing assignments came from this book. There's a humorous chapter about a brave courting his intended wife. During discussion of the chapter, students offered examples of dating and marriage customs from their cultures. Our class was silent as Helen, a Chinese student, described how her grandparents had arranged her marriage to the son of old friends; Helen was never alone with her prospective husband until after the wedding. Then an East Indian student from Trinidad explained that his parents' marriage was also arranged and that they had never met before the ceremony. This student had always appeared detached from class, so his joining the discussion was a breakthrough. An African American woman from Georgia described her parents' courting rituals, which illustrated that American patterns also varied according to the time and place. Her parents belonged to the same church and understood that they could only date and marry members of their own congregation.

HERNÁNDEZ: I remember seeing some of those compositions.

HAAS: A group of assignments evolved from this discussion. First, students interviewed older relatives or friends from their cultures about dating and marriage customs and wrote about these. Then students wrote compositions comparing their own dating customs with those described in the interviews.

HERNÁNDEZ: I read those.

HAAS: We helped students write in various rhetorical modes developed thematically. Trudy and I never decided that we wanted students to write narration, description or comparison, but all types of rhetorical modes flowed naturally from the topics.

SMOKE: The writing in my class was thematically organized around our readings and discussions.

HAAS: During planning, we decided we wanted students to write often.

SMOKE: My students wrote for at least twenty minutes each class meeting.

HAAS: I wanted students to experience all types of writing all semester, so throughout the term I encouraged them to write what Britton (1979) calls poetic, expressive, and transactional forms. I didn't rule out personal or poetic forms in favor of transactional writing.

SMOKE: I tried to do the same thing. My students decided what they wanted to write about and came up with their own questions, which also automatically prescribed the form of the pieces. By the way, my students also chose to write about marriage. There was one Muslim student who wrote about why she believed in arranged marriages and how she looked forward to her own.

During one of their first assignments, students role-played that they were Native Americans during the colonial period and discussed what had happened to them. Later they wrote about their feelings. A lot of anger came out.

HERNÁNDEZ: Yes, immigrants often have anger. Their anger stems from two sources: identification with a conquered people's resentment at being dominated and disappointment when discovering that the United States has not lived up to their image of freedom and equality.

SMOKE: I wasn't prepared for that. When they played the roles of Native Americans, students vicariously experienced oppression. They acted out the arrival of the Europeans. In their role playing, they had been living peacefully and suddenly they were forced to leave their homelands and families. They had to endure starvation marches on which many died and relocate to places where they were alone and alienated. The students drew upon their own experiences as immigrants.

HERNÁNDEZ: Right, I want them to relate this history to their own lives.

SMOKE: So even though they were writing as Native Americans, their own feelings of dislocation were coming through. There was a lot of anger, fear, and sadness.

HERNÁNDEZ: Yes, when a content course like mine that touches upon personal identity is presented through lectures, small discussion groups such as yours and Teri's are absolutely necessary.

HAAS: We know from our own experiences and from your study, Trudy, (Smoke 1988) and other research (Hirsch 1986) that nontraditional college students do not do well in large lecture courses.

HERNÁNDEZ: The large lecture course without small group sessions is not pedagogically sound. And a lecture course like mine that stirs up so many emotions must be combined with discussion groups.

HAAS: During the time we spent on the Native Americans, I developed an assignment similar to Trudy's. As one writing choice, I suggested that students imagine they were Native Americans and describe the scene and their feelings when they first saw the colonists. Students shared their curiosity and optimism; perhaps these are comparable to many immigrants' initial feelings about this country.

HERNÁNDEZ: Before they confront the problems.

HAAS: Of course, anger surfaced at other times. A student from Trinidad, for example, compared his problems with those of Chicanos. Many African Americans also related to the type of prejudice felt by immigrants of color.

SMOKE: I attended all of José's classes. My writing class followed his immediately and in my class we discussed the lectures, readings, and other relevant issues that emerged from the subject material. Sometimes I read difficult text material aloud. As a group, we created topics of mutual interest and then wrote about them.

HAAS: We also discussed the readings and the writing questions that José assigned. One student, Gabriella, construed José's question differently after discussing it with her group and rewrote her essay.

SMOKE: I think that's an important part of pairing, the collaborative thinking through of the lectures, readings, and other assignments.

HERNÁNDEZ: I agree, and especially as material is presented that touches on their own experiences. As the course continues, we focus on the long-term consequences of expansion and what this has meant for the people. The idea of migration is relevant to many of our students. The Native Americans and Chicanos were forced to leave their homelands. Economic reasons forced many Puerto Ricans to migrate to the United States. The whole process of social mobility in United States society becomes important to the course when we compare the experiences of one group with those of another. Toward the end of the course students become intrigued about why some Filipinos seem to be so successful in the United States today. This focuses upon the differences between peoples who have migrated and those who have immigrated. The Philippine Islands broke away, the Filipinos come as immigrants. Puerto

Ricans, whose island remained a territory, are migrants, moving back and forth without passports or visas. There are pluses and minuses to each experience.

HAAS: It seemed to our class that most of the conquered peoples have retained their cultures to some degree. You know, José, we enjoyed reading of the "salsa," or blend, of Puerto Rican Indian culture with that of African and European cultures.

HERNÁNDEZ: Teri, that's important because one of the objectives of this curriculum is to get away from the ranking of cultures as though they were baseball teams with first, second, and third place. What we tried to do was to impress students with the complexity of being conquered, the advantages as well as the disadvantages. Every matter of adversity can become an advantage.

HAAS: Didn't you have a Filipino professor talk to the class?

HERNÁNDEZ: He discussed what it meant to be part of a minority that is generally recognized as well-educated, affluent, and successful. Many of the Filipinos who come here are well-educated, nurses and doctors, for example, but they don't get jobs or income commensurate with their education.

SMOKE: "The Model Minority" (see Nash, this book) is the term used to describe the Asian minority's successes. But, as can be seen, Asians are only allowed to go just so far.

HERNÁNDEZ: Two Filipino women spoke to the class about specific problems related to gender. Many of the Filipino immigrants are women who face additional barriers to equality.

SMOKE: Although you might think it would, they said the crisis in nursing has not helped Filipino nurses who still suffer from cultural misreading. One of the speakers described a murder case where several nurses were accused of having killed patients. My students were fascinated because of the cultural biases. For example, these nurses in showing modesty would not meet the eyes of their interrogators and that was interpreted by the jury as a sign of guilt; to say "yes," the nurses shook their heads from side to side instead of up and down, and that was also misinterpreted. The nurses were convicted, although eventually the verdict was overthrown. Again, their cultural patterns and the fact of their being from another country all worked against them.

HERNÁNDEZ: This is an important point because it illustrates that discrimination is also faced by the well-educated. This is eye-opening because some students believe that by getting a college education, they'll avoid discrimination. Even though they may be disappointed, they usually become more motivated to succeed.

HAAS: Speaking of eye-opening, I want to digress and mention two parts of the curriculum that my class found especially interesting.

One was a writing assignment that students developed after your discussion of the "Coqui," the frog that in Puerto Rico is a symbol of defiance to oppression. Students wrote narratives about how the Coqui gained its reputation. The poems by Puerto Rican authors were also a success.

SMOKE: I think students reading this poetry realized that poems can be about real and even painful issues.

HAAS: Yes.

SMOKE: "Puerto Rican Obituary" by Pedro Pietri (1973) is a powerful poem that confronts very real issues such as employment, inferior housing, and competition among immigrants. My ESL students could strongly identify with those issues.

HERNÁNDEZ: As a social scientist, I'd rarely utilized fiction or poetry before we collaborated. But our discussions encouraged me to try, and I soon discovered that students learned from literature. Two short stories by Chicano writers, "Don Teodero" by Paul E. Martínez and "Angelina" by Rosalie Otero Peralta (Anaya and Marquez 1980), emphasize the value of tradition and the problems of stereotyping. I could talk abstractly in social science terms and never have as much effect as does a story of five pages.

HAAS: When I think of the outstanding experiences during this semester, I remember the stories, poetry, and dramatic events.

HERNÁNDEZ: "Maromas" from *Family Installments* (Rivera 1982) has all of the social science issues that I discuss: dropping out of school, social isolation, discrimination, segregation, and unemployment.

SMOKE: It also includes what it means to be successful or unsuccessful in the United States, the father's and mother's roles in the family. It even describes what happens when the boss comes to dinner. Very rich.

HERNÁNDEZ: Working class students immediately identify with this, but students who don't have working-class experience in the United States don't understand the story too well.

SMOKE: They may gain a useful new perspective. The Latino woman is so stereotyped in movies. José, you present a different point of view in these stories. You present traditional women, strong and capable, holding their culture together. This is a part of gender identity, recognizing that the woman's role was important.

HERNÁNDEZ: The woman's role in these cultures has been traditionally ignored by historians and social scientists.

Journals

HAAS: Can we talk about some of the writing assignments that we tried in our classes—journal writing, for example? My students wrote several pages each week about topics of interest from José's class or mine. I suggested they interpret this broadly and also use the journals to question anything they didn't understand or agree with. These were sometimes the basis for class discussions; at other times I responded in writing or asked students to exchange journals and write to each other. Students didn't find this easy.

SMOKE: What wasn't easy, writing the journals or moving from the journals to discussion?

HAAS: Students claimed they didn't know what to write about. I took for granted that students would listen to José's lectures and then relate these to their own experiences. In my own journal, I modeled ways I did this, but unless we had discussed a subject and moved in class from the abstract to the individual experience, students did not relate their experiences to the lectures. I believe that the skills of making those connections is learned, and expressive talk is one important method of learning this.

SMOKE: If I wanted my students to focus on José's class in the journals, I'd ask very specific questions. For example, after José gave the first examination, I asked students what they thought of it. Many were very troubled because it consisted of true-and-false and multiple-choice questions. They claimed that for ESL students, these are particularly difficult. The addition of one word such as "not" could change the whole meaning of the sentence. If they tried to read quickly or to translate, they might lose the word or forget that the sentence had a negative in the beginning. A tense could also change the meaning of the question completely. After students explained all this in their journals, I discussed it with José, and he added more writing questions to his other tests. The journals were helpful in allowing students a voice in course development. I like the journals to be exploratory.

HAAS: For students to write about themselves for interested readers seems especially important for nontraditional students who may feel isolated at the college.

SMOKE: The power of journals is in giving students a voice. My students who use the journals the most are those who frequently are reluctant to speak in class. This reminds me of an experience I had in José's class. Claudio, one of my students from Haiti, was sitting next to me during José's class, and he had a question. He asked me to ask the question for him, and I suggested he do it. He wrote out his question and asked if I thought it sounded right. I read it and said it was fine. But Claudio sat there and never asked his question. Later he explained he was afraid of making a mistake, of not "sounding right." This happens all the time. ESL students sit there, bursting with questions they are fearful of asking. The journal gives them that voice.

HERNÁNDEZ: This is a problem in large lecture classes. Students do not speak up even after I ask for questions. It's inhibiting for them to speak in a room of one hundred students and with limited time.

SMOKE: Our students may not know how to act in large lecture courses. They don't know what students are expected to do—when to ask questions, what type of questions. This is all learned behavior and can be very intimidating.

HAAS: According to Freire, poor people learn to practice silence in response to their feelings of powerlessness over their lives (1988). They might regard college as another institution in which they have no control.

SMOKE: ESL students may have additional problems, depending upon their culture's perception of correct classroom behavior.

Collaboration

HAAS: I felt that the collaboration between the teachers was important. We met several times during the summer and planned how to integrate courses. José shared his course materials (Hernández 1989), and we discussed our tentative plans for the writing courses. During the semester, we all met for lunch weekly, and Trudy and I met each day after our classes, analyzed them, and discussed our assignments.

SMOKE: I think one positive change would be to have even more discussion over writing assignments that José will give his class.

HAAS: Another interesting aspect of our collaboration was my discussion of individual students with José.

HERNÁNDEZ: Yes.

HAAS: I realized how differently we perceived some students. For example, one student whom I construed as lazy, José described as working hard. I suspect that this student's behavior in my class was a defense, perhaps, because of his second language problems.

HERNÁNDEZ: I was also surprised by your enthusiasm for another student's composition that you brought to one of our meetings. When I looked at his name, I recollected a mediocre student who had appeared bored during lectures. So we gain new views of students when we collaborate.

HAAS: I was reminded of my subjectivity.

HERNÁNDEZ: Yes. I had the exact same number of students in my morning and afternoon sections, but throughout the semester I felt I related better to the afternoon class because they were more articulate and appeared more involved in the topics, while the morning people seemed less interested. But I was amazed when I read the final examination essays that brought together all the substantive themes. The morning students did extremely well. Body language can be deceptive.

SMOKE: This brings up something that we should try to incorporate next semester. We should have a counseling component linked to our classes. Students may not be aware that body language suggests certain feelings, such as boredom. Maybe the student is not bored but confused. Certainly it could be useful to discuss students' body language with them and make them more aware of the way it's perceived by others.

HAAS: Another issue that should be mentioned is that we needed a lot of flexibility for this collaboration. While I planned the curriculum before the semester began, I needed to revise it and allow time for lessons that came out of discussions.

SMOKE: Yes, for example, students this term became very interested in maps. They didn't know that Spain was a part of Europe, but thought Europe was a separate country. And when José lectured about the British coming to the United States, a few Asian students who had never heard of the British in Great Britain, mistook the word "British" for "Buddhist" and misunderstood an entire lecture.

HERNÁNDEZ: I certainly changed my curriculum after talking to you. For example, I now include an initial section on geography.

SMOKE: Students enjoyed knowing where places are and seeing the possible relationships between peoples. Asian students, for example, saw physical similarities between themselves and Native Americans. They began to understand this after José's references to migrations over the land bridges between Asia and North America, information they had never known.

HERNÁNDEZ: Yes, at Trudy's suggestion, I offered more of an introduction to the origin of human beings, so that students understood the human race is one. Social differences are a product of family genetics and the environment.

HAAS: Another change precipitated by our collaboration was José's perception of writing. He began with the idea that he could help developmental students if he didn't assign writing until late in the term. Through our conversations, José came to understand composing as a way of learning.

HERNÁNDEZ: Yes, in the beginning my model was to prepare students to learn successful behavior for social science courses which often use short answer tests. I also believed that students would have an advantage by first taking objective tests and slowly moving toward essays. During our collaboration, I began to ask students to write informally and I responded in writing, so they understood if their comments were effective or missed the point. At first, some students only turned in a sentence or two, thinking that was enough, but when they realized that I preferred exploration to a quick answer, their next compositions changed radically. Students became much more expansive when they knew I was commenting only on their ideas.

SMOKE: We tried to emphasize the same thing. Although we all recognize that students must write correctly in order to complete college, we believe that working out meaning is of primary importance, and as students reformulate meaning, form may also improve (Mayher, Lester, and Pradl 1983).

HAAS: We must help students understand that we are interested in their meaning and not just their errors of form. Many developmental writing students believe that it doesn't matter what they say as long as grammar and spelling are okay. This may limit students' formulation of meaning.

SMOKE: I wanted to mention other ways our collaboration changed me. First, I allocated more time for student talk. At the beginning of the semester when I taped my classes, I found myself talking more than I thought.

HAAS: What did you do?

SMOKE: I forced myself to stop talking and let students talk more so that I could find out what they knew. Before this I had made certain assumptions about what I thought students weren't getting, but sometimes I was completely off. Students may have been having problems, but these were different from what I had supposed. So I changed in that regard. I also gave students a lot more flexibility to write about subjects they were interested in, to create their own questions. I organized the class as a workshop and went over each paper individually with the author. Students received immediate feedback.

HAAS: When did you intervene in the process?

SMOKE: Right after their first drafts. Also, many times I wrote with the class and shared my writing with them. Nick, the peer tutor, wrote and shared his writing (see appendix to this chapter). I found it enormously helpful to have Nick in my class full-time, although at first I was not entirely comfortable with a stranger in my class.

HERNÁNDEZ: I felt the same way at first with Trudy coming to my lectures.

HAAS: During the course of our collaboration, I also changed. I really enjoyed learning about new subjects.

SMOKE: That's true of me, also. I felt I learned a lot.

HAAS: Students gained more responsibility in my class. As Trudy said, we teachers talk too much even when we think we're being quiet. But last semester, students came from José's class to mine, and they were often stimulated by his lectures. Since I didn't really know what had happened in a specific discussion, they had to explain their ideas. Often, when students had questions they helped each other. My limited knowledge helped students become collaborators.

SMOKE: I felt that I was a learner throughout the semester, and I think that's very exciting.

HAAS: Before we discuss the results of this project, I wish to mention my gain. As a developmental writing teacher, I sometimes felt on the outskirts of the academic community, just as my students do. I felt less isolated while working with Trudy and José.

SMOKE: I agree.

HERNÁNDEZ: This has been a rewarding experience for me to collaborate with other faculty members for the first time.

SMOKE: Collaboration enhanced our teaching, our relationships with our students, and set up a model that carried into the classroom. During the first week of school, all of my students grouped themselves according to race or nationality: Asians sat in one clump, Latino in another clump, and Haitians in still another clump. By the end of the semester, they were integrated. They could extend their trust because they found they had similar backgrounds and shared many problems. If there were more collaborative efforts, faculty might find they could learn from each other and their students would follow their model.

HAAS: Yes, also students became friendly earlier on since they attended two courses together. They formed a community that had special social relationships. This may be especially helpful for nontraditional students at the beginning of their college careers.

Results

SMOKE: We have just discussed some of the anecdotal evidence that demonstrates the success of linking these courses. We also have some statistical support. One hundred percent of my students passed José's course and also passed the CUNY Writing Assessment Test that is used as a final for the writing course. And, as I mentioned, many were multiple repeaters of ESL writing, so this was a real achievement for them.

I gave them a reading assessment test at the beginning of the semester and their average reading level as that time was 7.5. One of the students had a 4.8 reading level. By the end of the semester, the average had gone up to 9.6 and the student with the 4.8 had jumped all the way up to 9.1. Now, I was not teaching reading in any way other than that students were reading real material, discussing the vocabulary, and getting repetition of the same words over and over in their textbook. In the beginning of the semester, many of my students didn't know what the word "conquered" meant, but by the end they knew that and many other words that related to sociology, anthropology, and history.

HAAS: So their vocabulary increased?

SMOKE: It increased dramatically. Also their comprehension increased because of reading sophisticated material that they were motivated to understand. They discussed and wrote about these same issues.

HAAS: My students also were successful, although they're too small a sample to make any generalizations. Seventy-five percent passed the Writing Assessment Test. Over 80 percent of these students passed José's course.

SMOKE: Those are good results, Teri.

HAAS: José, did you find any difference between the developmental students who were paired with our courses and other students?

HERNÁNDEZ: Yes, I did a preliminary analysis. I compared the grades of students in the paired courses with those who were not—all developmental students—and found that people in the paired courses got higher grades.

HAAS: Pairing courses helps students develop their writing because they are writing in both courses about subjects they're interested in, real college subjects, and doing different types of writing. There have been other successful models—a literacy curriculum developed at the College of the Bahamas (Fiore and Elsasser 1987), the UCLA project (Snow and Brinton 1988), and the Freshman Workshop Program at College of Staten Island (Benesch 1988).

SMOKE: Students really liked the course. At the end of the semester, I asked students if they'd recommend the course to friends. Every one of them said they'd tell friends to take the paired courses. They all felt they were receiving more than before, special treatment.

HAAS: Most of my students also liked the paired courses. I think we all agree that is reason enough to continue.

Appendix

Talking With a Peer Tutor

At the end of the semester, writing teachers Teri Haas and Trudy Smoke recorded this interview with their peer tutor, Nick Tscouchlarakis, an undergraduate who attended José Hernández's course, tutored in Trudy Smoke's class, and held discussion groups with students from both paired writing courses in the writing center.

SMOKE: What made you first get involved in this project, Nick?

NICK: I knew I could use the social-science course credit for my requirements.

HAAS: Did you know what the course was about?

NICK: I heard about it while I was tutoring at the writing lab. I got an idea from the course catalog. I knew, also, that I'd be working as a tutor for students from other classes and I'd probably be working with a teacher. I didn't know Trudy except once when she role-played with us in the writing lab last year. Later on, though, I realized that I had to do more work than I originally thought.

SMOKE: How much more work did you have to do?

NICK: For Professor Hernández's course, I read everything twice, I took notes, revised them, and made them into an outline. I also taped all the lectures.

HAAS: Why did you have to do everything twice?

NICK: It was hard to remember everything, and when I started—before we had that talk about closed and open questions—I thought, I'm a tutor now. I have to know what's going on. I have to know as much as the teacher because the students will expect a lot of answers from me. That's how I felt in the beginning, so I started reading and writing more.

HAAS: You did this because of your new responsibility?

NICK: Yes, it wasn't so much getting a better grade, but I was scared of not knowing enough.

SMOKE: Nick, I noticed that during the semester you changed. Did you feel that in any way?

NICK: One way I know I changed was because Teri kept telling me I shouldn't be giving students the answers, but it should be more like having a friendly talk about what we heard in class. So I changed and my outlines changed, too. First, they were like statements, and then I changed them to questions, and the questions were general sometimes.

HAAS: Can you give an example?

NICK: Yeah, in the beginning I'd say. "When was Puerto Rico conquered by the U.S.?" I would expect one answer, the date. And I'd have the date on my outline. But later on I'd say: "What do you think happened to the crops in Puerto Rico during this period?" And we'd talk and I would never give them the answers.

HAAS: Even if you felt they hadn't really answered correctly?

NICK: Well, I would always add something at the end, but usually I'd just tell them the page where they could find it.

SMOKE: Do you feel you learned anything during the semester?

NICK: I use what I learned in Hernández's course as background for my other studies. I also learned that the tutor shouldn't be too specific. In the beginning, I gave them answers, so they were satisfied. Sometimes the students just took my ideas and didn't add their own interpretations.

SMOKE: Doesn't that say something about students feeling insecure?

NICK: I was insecure in the beginning, too.

SMOKE: How did you get more secure?

NICK: By reading and talking. I was doing more talking than the other students. After a while, I tried to get them to do more talking, but I don't think I succeeded as much as I tried.

SMOKE: I have that problem, too. Do you, Teri?

HAAS: Talking too much? Yes, absolutely.

NICK: Yeah, I know, plus I was working so hard. I was reading my notes twice and writing them over and listening to Dr. Hernández's lectures which I taped.

HAAS: Did you always tape lectures?

NICK: No, just in Professor Hernández's course because I was the tutor. Now I tape other teachers' lectures, too.

SMOKE: Do you think we should suggest to students that they tape lectures?

NICK: You could suggest it, especially for students who have problems with note-taking.

HAAS: Did you show them your notes?

NICK: Yeah, I always showed them my notes.

HAAS: Did that help them?

NICK: Yes, I thought they might pick up the idea of being more specific and writing down more of what the teacher said.

SMOKE: Nick, do you remember in the beginning of the semester, we showed students our notes and they showed us their notes? Some of them had nothing, and others tried to write down every word and missed major points. After a while they began to improve a little.

HAAS: Nick, do you remember anything special from Professor Hernández's class?

NICK: Well, I had a negative idea about Puerto Ricans. I was a little bit unfair, not that much. But I lost that by listening to Professor Hernández, who was great, and, also, this was the first time I learned to communicate with a teacher.

HAAS: How did you learn to communicate?

NICK: Sometimes I had questions and I'd write them down and give them to him and he'd return the answers at the next meeting. When I had questions about the tests, I'd talk to him in his office and find out ideas about the answers. I also told the other students to do that.

SMOKE: How did you change in your feeling toward Puerto Ricans?

NICK: It was a history lesson. It brought me down to earth. I also learned from the films.

HAAS: What were the films?

NICK: One was about the Chicano community and another about how the Puerto Ricans were being exploited. I felt like they didn't deserve this, and if they're negatively stereotyped it's because we want them to be inferior. So I realized people are not always like they seem. In general, I started talking to Puerto Ricans more. Also, the things we did in Trudy's class helped. Reinaldo brought in a tape of the author reading his poem.

SMOKE: You mean "Puerto Rican Obituary" (Pietri 1973)?

NICK: That was good because we heard the author's tone of voice when he read it, and Reinaldo also brought in his dance videotape. We also saw some of the movie *West Side Story* (Robbins 1961) and noticed the stereotypes. Four or five students in Trudy's class were Latinos, and they explained how they felt. Some of the Haitian and Chinese students found they had similarities of culture. In the writing lab, one of the students was of Puerto Rican descent. His mother knew about the *jíbarros,* the farmers in Puerto Rico. Later on, he told me not to have such a closed mind and we started talking about that. He brought up his experiences. I brought up my experiences as an ESL student. That was really a help to me.

SMOKE: How old were you when you came here from Greece?

NICK: I was ten.

SMOKE: Did you speak English?

NICK: No, I didn't.

HAAS: How did you learn?

NICK: At school.

HAAS: Were you in an ESL class?

NICK: No, a regular third grade, but, also, I took a special program.

SMOKE: Before, we were talking about the Rodriguez (1981) book you're reading. Did you have to give up your culture, do you think?

NICK: Yeah, I did lose some. I changed, but I didn't lose everything. So I could understand how our students felt, too.

References

Anaya, R. A., and A. Márquez, eds. 1980. *Cuentos Chicanos.* Albuquerque: University of New Mexico Press.

Benesch, S. 1988. Linking content and language teachers: Collaboration across the curriculum. In *Ending remediation: Linking ESL and content in higher education,* ed. S. Benesch. Washington, DC: TESOL.

Black Elk and J. G. Neihardt. 1979. *Black Elk speaks: Being the life story of a holy man of the Oglala Sioux.* Lincoln: University of Nebraska Press.

Britton, J., T. Burgess, N. Martin, A. McLeod, and H. Rosen. 1979. *The development of writing abilities (11–18).* Urbana: NCTE.

Brown, D. 1972. *Bury my heart at Wounded Knee: An Indian history of the American West.* London: Pan Books.

Dean, T. 1989. Multicultural classroom, monocultural teachers. *College Composition and Communication.* 40: 23–37.

Deloria, Jr., V. 1969. *Custer died for your sins: An Indian manifesto.* New York: Macmillan.

Fiore, K., and N. Elsasser. 1987. "Strangers no more": A liberatory literacy curriculum. In *Freire for the classroom: A sourcebook for liberatory teaching,* ed. Ira Shor. Portsmouth, NH: Boynton/Cook.

Freire, P. 1988. *Pedagogy of the oppressed.* trans. Myra Bergman Ramos. New York: Continuum.

Hernández, J. 1989. *Conquered peoples in America.* First Developmental Edition, New York: Department of Black and Puerto Rican Studies, Hunter College.

Hirsch, L. M. 1986. The use of expressive function talk and writing as a learning tool with adult ESL students across the curriculum. Ph. D. diss., New York University, New York.

Laviera, T. 1985. *AmeRican.* Houston: Arte Publico Press, University of Houston Press.

Mayher, J., N. B. Lester, and G. Pradl. 1983. *Learning to write/Writing to learn.* Portsmouth, NH: Boynton/Cook.

Momaday, N. S. 1969. *The way to Rainy Mountain.* Albuquerque: University of New Mexico Press.

Pietri, P. 1973. Puerto Rican obituary. New York: Monthly Review Press.

Rivera, E. 1982. *Family Installments: memories of growing up Hispanic.* New York: Wm. Morrow.

Robbins, J. 1961. *West Side Story.* Mirisch/Seven Arts.

Rodriquez, R. 1981. *Hunger of memory.* Boston: Godine.

Smoke, T. 1988. Using feedback from ESL students to enhance their success in college. In *Ending remediation: Linking ESL and content in higher education,* ed., S. Benesch. Washington, DC: TESOL.

Snow, M. A., and D. M. Brinton. 1988. Content-based language instruction: Investigating the effectiveness of the adjunct model. *TESOL Quarterly* 22 (4): 553–74.

Notes on Contributors

Elsa Auerbach is Assistant Professor in the Bilingual/ESL Graduate Studies program at the University of Massachusetts at Boston and Coordinator of the Bilingual Community Literacy Training Project. She is co-author with Nina Wallerstein of *ESL for Action: Problem-Posing at Work* (Addison-Wesley, 1987), a Freire-inspired ESL textbook for the workplace. In addition, she had published numerous articles on critical perspectives on adult ESL and family literacy in such publications as *TESOL Quarterly* and the *Harvard Educational Review*. She was Coordinator of the UMass/Boston English Family Literacy Project from 1987 to 1990.

Sarah Benesch is Assistant Professor of English and ESL Coordinator at the College of Staten Island, City University of New York. She is editor of and a contributor to *Ending Remediation: Linking ESL and Content in Higher Education* (TESOL, 1988) and co-author of two ESL composition textbooks, *Academic Writing Workshop* (Wadsworth, 1987) and *Academic Writing Workshop II* (Wadsworth, 1989). She has made frequent presentations at TESOL, CCCC, and NCTE on such topics as using computers to teach writing, linking content and language, and collaborative learning.

Juan Cartagena is a civil rights attorney and the legal director for Puerto Rico's Department of Puerto Rican Community Affairs. In representing Puerto Ricans and Latinos throughout the Northeast, he has brought suit on behalf of workers fired for speaking Spanish on the job, parents who seek bilingual education for their children, and voters who demand bilingual assistance at the polls. A regular speaker at many forums and debates addressing language rights and English only issues, Mr. Cartagena has also written a number of related articles.

Carole Edelsky is Professor of Curriculum and Instruction at Arizona State University. She is the author of *Writing in a Bilingual Program: Había Una Vez*, published by Ablex in 1986. Her work on the writing of bilingual children has also appeared in *Research in the Teaching of English*, *TESOL Quarterly*, and *Southwest Journal of Linguistics*. Her research on gender and conversational structure has appeared in *Language in Society*. A recent study of gender and language in the context of televised political debates will soon be published in *Journal of Language and Social Psychology*.

Georges E. Fouron received his Ed.D. in language, literature, and social studies from Teachers College, Columbia University, in 1984. His doctoral thesis was a study of Haitian immigrants' processes of adaptation to life in New York. He is currently Assistant Professor in the Social and Behavioral Sciences Program at the State University of New York at Stony Brook. He has published numerous articles on black immigrants' identity in and adaptation to the United States. His forthcoming book, *Dependency and Labor Migration: Haiti in the Sphere of Global Capitalism* (Duke University Press), analyzes Haitian immigration and emigration from the perspective of economic and political globalism and dependency.

Teri Haas is Assistant Professor in the Department of Academic Skills, Hunter College. She teaches developmental writing and directs a writing lab. She has presented at CCCC and published articles in *The Writing Center Journal* and *The Writing Lab Newsletter*. She is currently doing research on how college writing centers support multicultural students.

José Hernández is Professor and Coordinator of Puerto Rican Studies at Hunter College. Dr. Hernández is developing a textbook, *Conquered Peoples in America*, on nineteenth-century U.S. expansion and the experience of Puerto Ricans, Native Americans, Chicanos, Hawaiians, and Filipinos. Formerly he was Director of Research at the Latino Institute in Chicago and Professor of Sociology at the University of Wisconsin, Milwaukee. Dr. Hernández is the author of *Puerto Rican Youth Employment* and other publications about the educational and employment situations of Puerto Ricans in the United States. He also directed a U.S. Commission on Civil Rights project that produced a report, *Social Indicators of Equality for Minorities and Women*.

Samuel Hernandez, Jr., is a student at the College of Staten Island and a member of the United States Coast Guard.

Sarah Hudelson is Associate Professor of Curriculum and Instruction at Arizona State University. A former elementary teacher, her research interests include focus on the acquisition and development of reading and writing in bilingual children, in both a native language and in English as a second language. Her most recent publication is a monograph, *Write On: Children's Writing in ESL*, published by the ERIC Clearinghouse for Languages and Linguistics and Prentice-Hall/Regents in 1989.

Loren McGrail is an ESL resource specialist at the Adult Literacy Resource Institute. She was a participating teacher in the UMass/Boston English Family Literacy Project in 1986-1988. She is co-author of *Talk Shop: Participatory Approaches to ESL* (UMass/Boston, 1989).

Philip Tajitsu Nash is Assistant Professor of Law at the City University of New York Law School. He co-hosts a regular radio show, "Supreme Court Watch," on WBAI-FM. He has written and spoken extensively on ESL issues to college and Asian American community audiences. Professor Nash serves on the boards of the Asian American Legal Defense and Education Fund, the National Pacifica Radio Foundation, and The Nation Institute's Supreme Court Watch Project.

Trudy Smoke is ESL Coordinator in the Department of Academic Skills at Hunter College. She is the author of two textbooks, *A Writer's Workbook* (1987) and *A Writer's Worlds* (1990), both published by St. Martin's Press. She was a contributor to *Ending Remediation: Linking ESL and Content in Higher Education* (TESOL, 1988). Professor Smoke has presented at many conferences, including TESOL and CCCC.

William Waxman is Principal of the James A. Garfield School in Revere, Massachusetts, and supervises student teachers at Salem State College. Under his direction, the Garfield School has won many awards, including commendation by the National Chapter of Phi Delta Kappa as a school with exceptional curriculum and discipline. From 1986 to 1989, Mr. Waxman served as a member of Governor Dukakis's Advisory Board on Refugee Resettlement.